Dear Dan,

To you,
with Gratitude
& Love,

Michèle Mirini Blurro

A Handful of Raisins in an Otherwise Empty Room

A Journey from Tragedy to Joy

Michèle Misino de Luca

a memoir

A Handful of Raisins in an Otherwise Empty Room
A Journey from Tragedy to Joy

www.micheledeluca.art
Cover art: Michèle Misino de Luca

Printed in the United States of America
Hardcover ISBN: 9781956019889
Paperback ISBN: 9781956019896
Ebook ISBN: 9781956019902

Canoe Tree
Press
Canoe Tree Press
4697 Main Street
Manchester Center, VT 05255

Canoe Tree Press is a division of DartFrog Books

Disclaimer

This book is a memoir. Since we all live in our private paradigms, our private dramas, I have described situations and scenarios, people and personalities, memories and suppositions, as seen through my eyes, heard through my ears, and felt through my heart. No part of this book is intentionally fictitious and I would not swear to its complete veracity. It is just how I remember things.

Some of the names of just a few of the people in this memoir have remained the same. These beautiful people have been so intrinsic to my life, it is as if they are a part of me. It is my task only to love them and honor them for all their humanity. I am utterly grateful to have known them.

I have changed the names of some other very good people who have played their distinctive roles in my life. They deserve, at the very least, their privacy. They deserve forgiveness for their mistakes and accolades for the brilliance of being who they were in this world of conflict and confusion.

Finally, I have changed the names of other people simply because they were terrible human beings who do not deserve to have their names inscribed anywhere but on their tombstones. But that is not up to me.

I kept names and changed names. I've told my truth, but not the truth. That is all I can do.

This book is dedicated to
Aurea Nellie Feliciano
one of the best human beings I have ever met.

And thank you to my parents,
Pete and Toni DeLuca,
the good people who made me.

Table of Contents

Foreword

In reading Michèle's memoir, I was blown away by the thoughtful and beautiful insights into our shared human reality. In writing her memoir, Michèle has found herself and her freedom at last. Her higher spiritual being has broken free from the shackles of her past, unbound by the limitations of remembered traumas. This is the story of how the author of this book became the author of her own life.

Fifty years ago, I met Michèle in high school. It was 1971. Little did I know I was meeting my life-long friend. I was a junior; she was a "super-senior," someone who had to complete a second senior year of schooling before being granted a high school diploma. She was dragging a troubled childhood behind her, unseen by the rest of us, like the proverbial convict's ball and chain. Except she was the victim, not the criminal, and did not deserve to be shackled to the dark history of her early years. Instinctively I sensed her inner struggles and knew they had a stranglehold on her psyche. Like tuning forks brought together on the same frequency, they resonated with my own personal traumas. Yet I could sense her inner strength, too.

Michèle was cute, vivacious and had an infectious giggle. Sitting behind her in our homeroom class, I did what any mischievous teenage boy would do who had an attractive girl sitting in front of him. I teased her. At times, mercilessly. Like so many young people, then and now, we were a couple of confused kids wanting to be accepted and liked by our peers, but lacking the necessary self-esteem to accept and like ourselves first. We found in each other a kindred free spirit, neither of us knowing where we were headed in life or what we wanted to be.

We graduated high school. I went on to college and lost touch with Michèle for a time. Michèle began her journey towards finding her inner truth, diving into as many interesting life encounters as she could fast discover.

All the while, the greater world around us was spinning out of control: terror at the Munich Olympics, the breakup of The Beatles (sigh!), the tragic loss of life at home and abroad (Kent State, Viet Nam with friends and brothers not returning home from military service), the shadow of the Watergate burglary and disgrace of the President, and on and on it went.

We were restless, brave and adventuresome. We each took off in different directions, gallivanting around the country.

When my life fell apart after I lost my marriage, my business and both parents in a short period of time, Michèle was there to lift me back up in more ways than I can express. She reminded me of who I was and helped me transform my life. I am forever grateful for her undying love and support.

I also witnessed Michèle's many changes over time. She knows what it feels like to go hungry. She knows what it means to be broke, but she was never broken by the pain inflicted upon her by others. Michèle has thirsted for honest human-to-human interaction her entire life, remained open to possibilities and has been a catalyst for the awakening in others of their higher spiritual selves.

Michèle's proclivity for originality brought her much success as a children's entertainer in the San Francisco Bay Area. Known as Buki the Clown, her ongoing work is a testament to the reality she creates. She brings joy to others.

I have also been witness to her ability to forgive. Remarkably, despite past grievances, she never abandoned her mother, whose descent into debilitating dementia over many years was counterbalanced by the depth of Michèle's devotion. A dutiful, loving daughter, she took care of her ailing mother to the very end.

To truly know oneself has always been Michèle's foremost goal: who she is in the world, where she stands in relation to her fellow human beings, and what her true worth is as a person of influence. An understanding of that self-knowing appears in every chapter of this book, illuminating thoughts that, if you allow them to enter your mind, can be painfully insightful into the human condition and equally uplifting and inspiring as anything you can imagine.

This ever-striving for truth, both personally subjective and universally objective, demonstrates the authenticity that her words convey. Being true to oneself is what fills these pages.

This memoir is one more way to be fully present in her life and in the lives of others. It is a release from the grief for the lost little girl whose only hope out of sadness was in a handful of raisins.

You will be forever enriched by the simple wisdom, witticism and artful playfulness that Michèle has infused in her writing. I am proud of Michèle's many accomplishments and honored to call her my oldest and dearest lifelong friend.

Glenn Biren
Fishkill, New York
July 15, 2021

Preface

This book is not about the past, despite the fact that I am telling the stories of my past. My early years were fraught with challenging situations, as perhaps was yours. I adopted certain strategies for survival when I felt seriously threatened. Some of those threats were psychological. Some were physical. At such times, some people react by becoming outgoing. Some hide. Some run away. Some fight. I did what I did, stuck in the moment, cemented into a present in which I had no control. I was a victim of circumstance at age 5. I had no choices. I went where the grown-ups took me, screaming and crying or disappearing into a deep dark cavern in my soul. When I emerged, I became a survivor. However, a survivor claims the challenging experience as part of their identity. They are, figuratively, signing their name upon an incident in life in which they had no control, essentially claiming it as the source of who they are. I did that, until I realized that I had within me the power and desire to create myself based on the aspects of humanity I value most. So I gave up the idea of being a survivor. I am still evolving, noticing where each challenging event caused me to invent a strategy that defended me from life itself. Some of those strategies are still there, like automatic pilot, and I am grateful that they are. But strategies are designed in the past and block my experience of the Present. Who I want to be, who I am driven to be is a fully-alive soul motivated not by fear or defensiveness, but instead by inspiration. I want to feel deep-rooted compassion for everyone who crosses my path and in order to do so, I must be willing to forgive my own humanity, my own misdoing that stemmed from my attempts to survive. I want to bet my life on the deepest of depths possible, not the depths of misery, but the depths of Soul. Envisioning first the earliest of times when Life was just Life and I had no choice but to accept it, I want to grow deeper. I want to grow into an unknown, into a spirituality undefined by the outside world, and designed by the deeper soul that has looked at the world through my eyes since it was born.

Sometimes I see myself as a hero and I am grateful to my younger self for getting up, dusting myself off and continuing on my journey. But hero is not my self-definition. I strive to be in life so immersed in its creation, every step my own invention, that I cannot separate myself from life itself. I don't want to just experience life. I want to BE life.

Consider the musician who masters playing their scales, endeavors to understand the structure of the score, then practices playing it flawlessly per the composer's invention. Ultimately, the technique is there like the ground they walk upon. So immersed they become in the beauty of this expression, that they become the music, ascend from that technical ground until they are transformed into something else, something beautiful, something invented in the moment that has never been heard quite that way before.

That is who I strive to be. That artist. That creative. That alive. That present. This book is an effort and exercise in transformation and ascendence. I invite you to accompany me. I invite you to discover the journey of your own soul and ascend.

1

Beginning

When my mother was pregnant with my younger brother, she tried to commit suicide. Whether it was a call for attention made during a time of day when she knew my father would be returning to save her, or an actual attempt to end her life, no one will ever know. But clearly, it was an act of desperation.

She took all my father's meds, methodically taking the bottles from the medicine cabinet and swallowing their contents by the handful. Years later, when I was perhaps 13 or 14, she confided bits of the story to me when she wouldn't let me buy a particular brand of soap. Apparently the cops had mixed soap and water and made her drink it so she would vomit up the toxic contents of her stomach. *It was my father's fault*, of course. He just wouldn't get his act together. He couldn't keep a job and he would often lie, covering up the fact that he hadn't reported to work, but instead sat for the entire day in a movie theater. Back in those days, the mid-1950s, you could stay in the theater and watch perhaps three movies which they would play back-to-back over and over again. I imagine him in a stupor instigated by confusion, self-loathing and depression. You see, my father really wanted to be a good man, a good husband and a good father. There were times when he recognized his brilliance and his capabilities. He realized wholeheartedly that his intelligence far exceeded that of the regular joe, and he knew that the enterprise he would soon embark upon would be the answer. He could do it. He could do what no one else could. He was Peter DeLuca, the one and only, the Peter DeLuca who had been spoiled, raised with no sense of consequence, and the Peter DeLuca who could do no right. He would ride high on his newfangled strategy to make money and then, just days later, like an anvil dropped from the sky in a 50s cartoon, reality hit with a deep darkness in his soul. And then he just couldn't. He couldn't produce any result; he couldn't take the actions of a good husband and father. He couldn't look in the mirror without wincing that that shell of a man had returned to haunt him and taunt him with the truth: something was deficient in Peter DeLuca; no. More than deficient. Something was totally defective and utterly irreparable.

And it showed. Even walking down the street caused pangs of self-loathing and guilt as he desperately avoided the gaze of the passers-by for fear his unworthiness to be alive would be discovered. He felt his unworthiness advertise itself and he longed to disappear. Just disappear. He became a truant from work, choosing instead to hide himself in the dark and bury himself in the story on the screen, like a drug. There was no way to climb out of his body, climb out of his pain. So he anesthetized himself. In a sense he did go to work—the work of medicating himself within the cinematic unreality in an attempt to climb out of his body and for at least a few hours, escape the pain of being Peter DeLuca.

The story was (as my mother told it) he had pills to wake him up and pills to put him to sleep, pills to give him an appetite, and pills to quell it. Some of those pills had severe side effects and so he had more pills to counteract the side effects. That day, after Peter left for his escape route, she took them all. She couldn't face it anymore. This would show him what a weak man her husband was. Now he would know what real suffering was.

But he came home, found her, and the cops forced her to drink that horrid concoction of water and soap. She spent a few days at Bellevue. Humiliated.

The psychiatrist met with my mother, and then she met with my father. And according to my mother, the psychiatrist had told her that "that man can do nothing to help you, Toni. You need to accept that you are on your own."

This was the legacy she delivered to her kids. I was the only one who knew about the suicide attempt. Why she told only me, I will never know. But the Peter DeLuca she told us about had no backbone, owed money, spent money he didn't have on gadgets, and then (thankfully) had abandoned us by having a massive heart attack at age 41. Yes, even that was his fault, because despite the doctor's goading advice, he never stopped smoking cigarettes and overeating. At a time when he finally had a good job that he seemed to be able to show up for, had friends, and things were going a bit better, he left us, all four children and my mother.

I was 7 years old. My older brother was 11, my sister 10 and my younger brother, the one my mother had been pregnant with at the time of her suicide attempt, was 16 months old. There is more to this pea soup of a story, more twists and turns camouflaged by my mother's inability to face reality. When my mother made that suicide attempt, the child she was carrying was not my father's. In 1959, that was a big issue. It makes some sort of perverse sense that killing oneself was on the very very short list of ways to cope in such a situation. An abortion, one might say. Add to that, we were about to be evicted from an apartment that had been rented first by a great uncle for many many years, and then by us, what options could she have had?

I have to make assumptions here. I was 5 at the time of the suicide attempt. I remember some visits to the police station, where, in a corner, was a large wooden box of donated toys. They must have been donated. They were in very poor shape. I remember a naked doll with disheveled hair and only one arm. I remember being embarrassed for her and wishing I could fix her. Then there was the trip to the court. There was a big room. Within the room, a gated area... gated with wood and a rich woody smell. I realize now that this must have been an unused courtroom and the gated area must have been a jury box. There my older sister and brother and I rummaged through the treasures of toys, much better toys than they had at the police station, and much better toys than we had ever had the pleasure to have owned. We played there, sensing strangeness in these inescapable moments, a strangeness that seemed to envelop us with its own indistinguishable color, shape and smell. As we played innocently inside the strangeness of that jury box, judgment was rendered in the next courtroom over. Disposition was determined by others unbeknownst to us. Freedom was lost to us. Family was lost to us. Belonging was lost to us.

A lady came in and told my sister and me to come with her. I looked at my sister as we were well trained not to go with strangers. But my sister coddled me (when we weren't fighting) and I was confident of her judgment and her care of me. So we left with the lady and went for a long ride, two ladies in the front seat of the car and my sister and me in the back.

2

Josephine's

I sensed that something was weird. But my sister, Dorie, was there, and I was in her protection. Dorie always took care of me.

When we stopped in front of a house with a white picket fence, the lady in the passenger seat who someone had called a "social worker," said, "Michèle, come with me." I looked at Dorie and Dorie said, "it's okay, you can go." So I did.

The social worker lady opened the white picket gate and holding my little hand, she led me up the path, and up a couple of porch stairs. The door opened and a salt-and-pepper-haired lady invited us in. The social worker lady introduced me, "this is Michèle," and the salt-and-pepper-haired lady said, "My name is Mrs. O'Brian, but you can call me Mommy O'Brian." I stood there frozen. All I could think was, "I'm not going to call you anything. I have a Mommy!" And I never did.

They explained to me that I was going to live there for a while. How could that be? I just want to go home. I just want to be with my Mommy and Daddy and Gregory and Dorie. I just want to go home.

Of course I cried. I was 5 years old. I don't know if anyone had attempted to prepare me for this moment, but if they did, I don't remember it, and if they did, it was absolutely ineffective. I was in utter shock. How could this be? How could this be?

When we left our MacDougal Street apartment, I didn't know we weren't ever going back there. Suddenly, without explanation, we slept at different places. There was someone's apartment further up the street, an older couple who clearly were afraid of having a child with them who took me in. I stayed with these strangers one night. One long, lonely, frightening night. The old apartment must have had a bathroom down the hall for all the tenants to use, and I suppose it had been occupied. They brought out a pot for me to pee in and both the man and the woman stood and watched while I did. I cringed with embarrassment but could hold my pee no longer. I slept somewhere in that apartment, enshrouded in fear. What was happening?

Then there was Josephine's. My Mom, my brother, my sister and I stayed there for about a week. She had a two-room apartment somewhere in Greenwich Village, another old place, this one with a bathtub in the kitchen. Josephine would take baths there in sight of all of us and would walk around naked. We all felt embarrassed. She had a young baby, too. Sometimes my Mom would leave us with Josephine while she attended to some important errand. The distinctive aspect of Josephine's were the roaches. And the roaches. And the roaches. You could look on any surface at any time and see dozens and dozens. It was guaranteed that they crawled on you while you slept. I covered my whole head and most of my face while I slept. Josephine did not believe in using chemical bug spray. Nor did she try to stamp out the roaches, which would have taken hours just for a first round. She just lived with them.

Above the couch was a huge world map. One day, the scotch tape that held it finally gave way. The map fell, held now only by one corner. As the map slipped, it revealed the wall behind it, nearly a solid brown speckled by the fading white paint. It suddenly went into motion as thousands of roaches scrambled in all directions. Dorie and I watched in horror.

9

You can, at any time, invoke that horror again in any of us with two words… *"remember Josephine's?"*

Two weeks in the Morrisania sleep-away camp and two weeks in the Catholic sleep-away camp isolated Greg on the boy's side and Dorie and me in different cabins on the girl's side.

At some point we stayed in hotels, a week with my Mom and a week with Dad. We kids had been separated and staying with a different parent during part of that time. I have few memories of my father, but one is crystal clear in my mind. I was 5 and tiny for a 5-year-old, and still I considered a possible solution for this upheaval in our lives. "I know what the problem is," I proclaimed. My father looked at me with a quizzical expression I remember clearly to this day. He said nothing. I continued. "You think Mommy has all the money and Mommy thinks you have all the money. But there is no money!" He must have felt crushed.

Finally, the foster home. I am sure every grown-up involved considered Mrs. O'Brian's foster home a better option than where my siblings were forced to live. "You were lucky," I remember my mother saying when the family was finally reunited. "You got to live in a house with a family and not in an institution." Perhaps that is the truth, that this was some form of luck, a slight reflection of light in an otherwise dark, cold and shadowy nightmare. Perhaps that glimmer of luck showed up in each trauma of my young life. It is not that my cup was half full, it is just that within this half-empty vat, murky with its fill of solitude and sadness, was a drop or two of karmic pity. Certainly, in any challenging event of our lives, it could have been worse. A lot worse.

It could have been worse when Michael, the 17-year-old boy who lived up the street, and I used to meet behind the long row of garages and he would proudly display his penis just for me, as he held it and gently fondled it. Karmic pity bestowed itself upon me. He never touched me. On one occasion, he ejaculated and said, "you can drink that, you know." Karmic pity reminded me of an older brother who would tease and talk me into doing things…like eating an acorn. "*You can drink that, you know,*" Michael suggested. I responded, "*you do it.*"

Mrs. O'Brian did create a fit home. The food was healthy, albeit not what an Italian little girl had been used to. I went to bed at a more than reasonable hour, at 7:00 p.m., even when the sun was still out. Mrs. O'Brian gave me a handful of raisins as she tucked me in. Not the dentist's prescription, I am sure, but I made those raisins last and last. I tore each

11

one open with my baby teeth and slowly licked out the soft, sweet pulp. Then I chewed the remainder slowly, over and over again, one at a time, until I swallowed and started to lick out the pulp of the next one. It was the personal ritual of a 5 year old and it comforted me at a time when there was little else to comfort me.

Ten months later, when our family was reunited, it now included a new baby brother, only a few months old.

My sister told me that she had always felt guilty that she had told me it was okay to get out of the car and go with the social worker. She cried as she apologized. Not your fault, Dorie. Not your fault. No need to apologize. No need for forgiveness. Only gratitude. Only love.

3

My Father
Peter DeLuca

As my life reached its Autumn stage, my mother's was deep in her Winter. Nearly 90, she had dementia. I had to pack up her belongings, determine what to keep and what to give to a thrift shop, even as I lied to her and told her everything would be kept safely in my garage. Then, against her wishes but in accordance with her needs, I moved her into a board and care facility. There were a lot of books in her small one-bedroom apartment, but she would never read again. Her mind could not focus itself onto the page. So by going through her belongings, I was dancing with her slow death, the death of things she loved to do, as well as the death of the possibilities that life had offered her and she let just pass by. But this part of my story is not about Toni DeLuca. It is about Peter DeLuca.

Among my mother's things, among the old 45 records, I found what are called "Voice-O-Grams." These are the size of 45s, but play at 33-1/3 rpm. My Dad had made them in the late 40s, I believe, when many record shops offered these tiny recording booths, where for 60 seconds, you could record whatever you pleased.

I was 61 years old when I found them. My father was 41 when he died. My life had already exceeded his in length by 20 years. Now my father was just a faded stain in my mind. It was such a long time ago, so many experiences between then and now, so great a passage of time made being fatherless normal for me. I had so few memories. I could not bring his voice into my present mind; it was a sound lingering way in the background. Vague were my memories of him: singing, playing mandolin, biting his tongue as he concentrated. My Daddy's voice when he admonished me as we were taking a bus from New York City to Syracuse. How it embarrassed me! A voice way way in the background. Until the Voice-O-Grams.

The first recording (all of them about 57 seconds long) was part of an ária from La Traviata, the second, some Sicilian folk song, and the third, a monologue from Spartacus. His recital is professional and impeccable, until about two-thirds of the way through this short recording, he breaks character and says to someone, "wipe your mouth, Bud." The woman he says this to laughs, and I realize it had to have been my mother, probably way before their kids were born and perhaps even before they were married. My mother was probably 21 and if so, my father, 26.

At 7 years old, your father is the person who you run to to wipe your nose when your mother is not available to do so. While I remember my mother mentioning that my father had written poetry, she had none of it to share with me. Her stories about my father's failures far outnumbered and outweighed stories of his talents. She had little compassion for his weaknesses. Mostly, she had disdain.

Now I listen to my father's voice, singing opera, singing in a Sicilian dialect, probably a native tongue despite the fact that he was born in New York City. I listen to him being a perfect thespian, then breaking character, even if only for a few seconds, offering up a bit of the real Peter DeLuca as a young man, a playful young man with a sense of humor, toying with his young and lovely and then-supportive and hopeful fiancé. My Dad. A person. A person with character, talent, and personality: My father.

My father was an artist in many media, as I am. My father loved to make music, as I do. He played the mandolin. I do not. My father loved theater, as I do, and truthfully, as my mother did. But my mother loved to watch it and my father and I both wished to participate front and center. We wanted to play full out and be part of it. I am honored to be my father's daughter and I feel incredibly fortunate to have been able to build a bridge between all those artistic aspirations and the reality of my life. My father never was able to do that. He had to work a J-O-B. He had a family to support and did not see a path to the self-expression he was born to achieve.

My father more than likely suffered from bipolar disorder. My sister insists he must have had PTSD from his involvement in the war, and that may be possible, as well. His mother and her sister suffered from, and eventually died from, Huntington's Disease. Was that the source of his possible PTSD?

Huntington's Disease or (HD) is fatal. It is a genetic disorder that progressively breaks down the nerve cells in the brain. It deteriorates a person's physical and mental abilities usually during their prime working years and has no cure.

Dora Crocciola DeLuca, my paternal grandmother, was diagnosed with HD when she was in her late 40s. She was hospitalized in 1940 and died from complications due to HD in 1946. Her son, Peter DeLuca, was 26 at the time. How do you cope? How do you love and receive love from a mother whose brain and body are no longer her own? Symptoms of HD usually start with difficulty concentrating, memory lapses and depression, and develop into severe involuntary jerking (similar to Parkinson's), muscle rigidity and the inability to speak or even to swallow. Huntington's Disease is a horror.

Simply stated, her entire nervous system and her brain broke down, as she jerked and writhed involuntarily. She had personality changes. These symptoms would be hard enough to witness in a stranger, but how does a child, even a grown child, witness this deterioration and destruction in a mother, a loving mother who can no longer offer anything at all? And is this a predictor of his future? Might he have inherited the gene that causes HD, as well?

Peter DeLuca probably did have PTSD, exacerbating and exacerbated by behavior that it seems to me was so classic, so textbook bipolar. When he was manic he would imagine a new business he would start and in two weeks, possibly three, he would be rolling in dough. The mania was short-lived and the possibilities that mania inspired were quickly eviscerated by reality. He'd feel his peripheral vision shrink and his world grew dark. He'd now owe yet someone else a pile of money with no way to pay it back. Humiliation and depression overwhelmed him and drove him to his medicine, those dark movie theaters. He wanted to die. And at age 41, that wish was fulfilled.

My father's mother died a horrible death due to HD in 1946. Peter DeLuca married my mother on June 1, 1947. Sometime during this period, he served in the U.S. Army during World War II, returning home to study at New York University. He never completed his degree. Perhaps being in the army gave him a reprieve from witnessing the dissipation of his mother, and then enrolling in University gave him another. A reprieve or a distraction? What did life look like through those 26 year old eyes? Where did he find peace, or did he? Where might he have found true happiness? How did he have any time to digest his feelings of horror at this untimely and cruel loss of his mother? While his symptoms of bi-polar disorder and perhaps PTSD caused him great suffering and feelings of unworthiness, it may have also created a great distraction from what was really going on in his heart. He was, indeed, a talented saboteur of his own life circumstances.

When my younger brother, Steve, was 32 years old, and I, 38, he called me. He had received a strange phone call from a woman who had been a good friend to my father's sister, who had died from various causes, including HD. This strange woman had been asking questions in order to complete a family tree. You see, many of my ancestors on my father's side had Huntington's Disease. If my father had the gene (and we do not know if he did) then his offspring have a 50% chance of inheriting it. And if any of us have the misfortune of inheriting the gene, then we will more than likely get Huntington's. Steve thought this stranger's call was not only weird but intrusive. She was demanding information which he was reluctant to give to a cold caller. When he refused her requests for information, the woman became frustrated and blurted out, "Nevermind! You are not in the bloodline anyway!" Steve immediately called me to ask me if there was any chance he had a different father.

It was a very long three or four seconds before I answered. It seemed the cells in my body were vibrating and somehow I heard my own voice reply, "yes. It is possible." With just a bit of further inquiry to a cousin and then a conversation with my Mom, it turned out it was true.

The picture I had of the world fell apart, like a jig-saw puzzle shattering, its pieces thrown in all directions as it hit the floor. It took a couple of weeks of some kind of unconscious recovery of information before life began to feel at all normal again.

The biggest breakthrough, though, was of my father, Peter DeLuca. The man my mother had been so disappointed in as she tried her damnedest to hold the family together, despite his failings, had also been the man who took her back and accepted the child born out of an affair as his own.

Peter DeLuca was a big man, a forgiving man. Peter DeLuca was, Peter DeLuca is, my Father.

4

Uncle Frank

We all lived on MacDougal Street in Greenwich Village, 93 MacDougal to be exact. Across the street was a little grocery store. It was run by my Uncle Frank LoGusto. My memories of him go back to when I was three years old. I remember his character and his quirks. He was my great uncle, my father's uncle to be exact. Yet it was clear to all the family he was mine. Despite the fact that I had an older brother and sister, Uncle Frank had chosen me. Totally mutual. I was strongly bonded to him and he was always my advocate. He was a crusty old man who smelled of cigarettes. He smoked filterless Camels and the stench was all over him. He wore a grayed white shirt and tie, and a dark gray button-down wool sweater which was probably never washed. It was scratchy, but nowhere near as scratchy as his face which always sported some serious whiskers, even though he shaved every day. He had a leather strap on which he would sharpen his straightedge, mix his shaving soap and water in a little cup with his shaving brush. Whipping it first into a thick lather, he would spread the white lather all over his beard. He'd shave a stroke or two and then rinse the blade in the kitchen sink, looking into a small mirror that had been perched on a shelf. I would watch this daily ritual, and despite his fastidiousness, when he picked me up minutes later, his face was still scratchier than sandpaper. He was an elderly man with a stale odor of old man and cigarettes and despite his scratchy sweater and beard, I loved him. I knew I was safe in his company as he attended to the care of this 3-year-old. I also knew that all I had to do was ask and he would bend over backwards to fulfill my requests.

MacDougal Street was and still is a short street. If you walk north, you would arrive at Washington Square Park, just a block away. This is where my brother, my sister and I played when we weren't playing directly in front of the store.

If you walk halfway up the block, you would arrive at Frank & Tony's, a small candy store that sold newspapers, magazines, and of course, a wonderful selection of chocolate bars and other yummies that would entice any child. One day, my parents' friend Murray, a very skinny, funny and loving man whose visits delighted us children, took me up the block to Frank & Tony's. He asked me what I wanted and

I picked out Jujubes. I liked other candy better, but Jujubes would last a very long time and since it was so rare for us to have treats like this, I wanted the candy that would last the longest. "What else?" he asked. I thought of Greg and picked out some chocolate. "What else?" he asked again, and I picked out a candy I knew Dorie liked. He asked again and again, and once I knew that I, and each of my siblings, had two swe232391et items each, I told him it was enough. "Really?" he asked several times. "Really. Nothing else?" I answered until he believed me. I didn't want to be greedy.

One day, I had a craving for some candy and asked my Uncle Frank to buy me some. He handed me a dime and I set off the half a block to Frank & Tony's. Just as I arrived, mouth watering, and as I lifted my foot onto the step leading to the door of the candy store, a hand grabbed me. It was my mother's. She took the dime from me and gave it back to my uncle, scolding him that it was too close to dinner and he shouldn't spoil me like that. My plans were sabotaged.

We attended Our Lady of Pompei Catholic Church on Carmine Street and Sixth Avenue (now called the Avenue of the Americas). Our family was well-known there, and my Dad was part of the Fathers' Club. It was a very active Italian Catholic community and each year they performed a play on their stage. The stage was a full one, equipped with the appropriate theatrical curtain. The room was filled with folding chairs and my entire family including Uncle Frank attended. Someone sang a song called "Shoeshine Boy." I was completely enthralled. I did not know such a thing as theater existed. I was elated, transported out of the moment into this perfect and colorful scenario enchanting my ears and my eyes. As the musical ended I was catapulted back to the present moment seemingly with a bump. My world was profoundly altered. What was this? Something miraculous! Generally, I was a shy little girl who literally hid behind my mother's skirts, but today, I was compelled. I had to step onto that stage. Was it real there? Was there another world up there I never knew existed? How could I enter that magic? Ask Uncle Frank. Of course, I could always depend upon Uncle Frank. He and I marched toward the stage. Just as we reached the stage right steps, I felt this hand. Of course, it was my mother's. She never knew how deeply crushed I was that she dashed my intentions and deferred this dream. But I still remember it all these years later. Evidence enough, I think.

Uncle Frank was in his late 70s and needed cataract surgery. He had surgery on only one eye. His right eye was patched and all in all, his vision was not good. I volunteered at the age of 3 to lead my Uncle Frank safely across MacDougal Street, watching for cars. I was proud to take care of him. He had always taken care of me.

One evening, my father's sister and her family came to our apartment. My Uncle Frank was in his dark and dusty bedroom packing a suitcase. He told me he had to go with his niece, my Aunt Phyllis. Disbelief shook my world. I cried and I promised him that I would never forget him and that I would come see him as soon as I grew up. He placed his rosary beads in my hand….he had had those rosary beads since he was a young boy in Sicily. I knew he was as sad as I was and I knew, even as a 3-1/2 year old, that this should not happen. Decisions had been made by grown-ups, but not by him and not by me. I went back into the kitchen where the adults were gathered and I cried and I demanded they not take him. Then I demanded to go with him. My Aunt Phyllis leaned over me and in the kind of syrupy sweet voice that people often use to talk to young children, she said, "you don't want to go and leave your Mommy and Daddy, do you?" But I did. I declared that I did over and over, but no one would listen. Uncle Frank needed me. I was his eyes. I was his heart. But who would listen to the wisdom of a 3-year old? I just had to grow up. Then I could do the right thing. I promised I would come see him when I grew up, not understanding that I would be visiting his grave.

This was the first time that I had experienced something going truly wrong in life. Of course there were times when I had fallen; I had cried; I had cried unfair when Greg and Dorie didn't include me in some game or other claiming I was too young to play. But I had never known powerlessness like this. Reality was broken and I could do nothing about it.

5

Foster Home

I was not, not even for a moment, comfortable in Mrs. O'Brian's house. I was isolated and lonely. I longed for my Mommy, my Daddy and my older brother and sister. There was a 3-year-old girl whom the O'Brians had adopted, Mary, but she was not interested in playing with me, nor I with her. I was always the stranger, in the living room, at the dinner table, at every moment. My skin felt like it wasn't my own and I longed to disappear.

The foods they served at dinner were unlike any I was used to eating. For one thing, my family was Italian and both my parents were raised very Italian. For another, my family was financially broke. It was not uncommon for us to eat plain spaghetti, or spaghetti with just butter or a basic marinara sauce that my mother quickly cooked in her cast iron frying pan. To her credit, Mrs. O'Brian cooked balanced meals and I was expected to clean my plate. I remember trying to cram down some turnips. They seemed to burn my tongue. I was not a good eater anyway since my stomach could only accept a little bit of food at a time. I did not know how I was going to manage to eat all this, most especially those horrid turnips. All eyes were on me… Mrs. O'Brian's, her husband's, her son's and her daughter's. I was told I had to eat it, and eat it all. So I tried. And tried, and finally, thankfully, Mrs. O'Brian took pity on me.

Mrs. O'Brian woke me up to go to school and dressed me in some overalls. They were not my overalls; they were the clothes she kept for her foster child, always a girl, I think. Then she sat me down at the coffee table where some hot cereal waited, butter, milk included. I could barely stomach it, particularly a wheat cereal, which had a texture of sand and a strong flavor I could not escape. Depending upon which hot cereal was on that day's breakfast menu, I would either eat little or none of it and then was put on the school bus which stopped right in front of the house. I must give Mrs. O'Brian credit, for even though I don't remember her ever uttering a comforting word, she fed me well and tried to provide me with quality care. I remember her discussing my mother with a couple of her friends, disdaining of my mother's pregnancy when she couldn't even take care of the children she already had. I remember wishing I had a voice, an adult voice, to defend my mother and tell that Mrs. O'Brian how much I hated her and why.

28

Being on the school bus was just about the best part of my life at the foster home. I had never had a friend before. Gregory and Dorie were my only companions and had always been more than enough. But life here in this Bronx foster home was desolate. The silence deafened me when it was just Mary, Mrs. O'Brian and me in the house. But now, on this yellow school bus, was a little girl named Georgia. She had big blue eyes and curly light brown hair. She spoke with a lisp and she and I would giggle our whole ride to school every day. A little boy named Ira sat between us and Georgia and I would count off....one....two....three....simultaneously kissing him on each cheek just to watch his face redden as he giggled and blushed.

My father came to visit and gave me a copy of Robert Louis Stevenson's "A Child's Garden of Verses." I learned to read in my solitude, my first poem there being "The Swing." I can recite it to this day.

One Saturday, my father was supposed to visit. I sat by the window and eagerly waited for his arrival. Minutes were hours long, as I waited and I waited, my heart, at first, seemed swollen with joy and anticipation. Then little by little, it deflated, until Mrs. O'Brian came to get me, put me in some seersucker pajamas, gave me a handful of raisins and put me to bed. He never called and of course, as a barely 6-year-old child, I never received a reason for his nonappearance.

My mother did visit, however sporadically, and that is how I learned she was pregnant. She had a large round belly and wore a black top with a little white collar. She was probably six or seven months along.

There were kids in the neighborhood who played together. I had no clue how to join them. One day I tried. Diana, the oldest of the group, apparently was not at all enthralled by the idea of allowing me to join the group. She found a worm and as she held it on a stick, threatened to make me eat it. The other kids, about ten of them, clustered behind her, and she slowly walked toward me threatening, "Don't forget! You won't need to eat your meat tonight because you will have already had it." She spoke in a menacing voice and I was scared. I ran back to the foster home, through the white picket gate and into the house. I didn't see her or the other children again until the day I was to go home. I was only told the morning of my departure that I was, in fact, going home. Others knew. A man named Jimmy saw me sitting at an open window eagerly waiting to be picked up. "Good for you!" he said. "You're going home today!" "How did you know?" I asked innocently. "A little birdie told me," he answered.

Young as I was, I wondered what that little bird looked like and how it knew.

As I looked out the window I saw a small crowd of kids approaching the white picket fence. They told Mrs. O'Brian they wanted to see me and I nervously came out. I figured they wouldn't try to harm me with Mrs. O'Brian standing right there. Diana said she was sorry for what happened the other day. She said she and the other kids had pooled their money and she handed me a small bag of assorted candies. I was happy. I was going home.

All in all, Greg, Dorie and I spent about nine or ten months in foster care, and speaking for all of us, I would wager it was the loneliest time in each of our lives.

6

My Mother Toni DeLuca

There is a picture of my mother, Antonietta Misino, when she was about 4 years old. The sepia print is pretty clear, a dark-haired little girl in a camel's hair coat and brown beret. I saw that photo when I was about 4 and it seemed to cause my brain to turn upside-down in my head. When had I taken that picture? While in some ways I really looked like my Dad when I was young, there were days when I was the spitting image of my mother when she was a child.

Toni Misino was born on April 24, 1925. I have a lot more to say about her because she was in my life for a long time, unlike my father, who died when he was 41 and I was 7 years old. My mother who made it to 94 years of age succumbed to Alzheimer's one brain cell at a time. It started when she was about 88. I took care of her needs or made sure they got met. It was nearly impossible to interpret my loss of her as it was happening. At first, she was able to feel the fading of her mental abilities. How could I assuage her fears? All I could do was promise her that I would always be there, always take care of her. Ultimately it seemed sacrilegious to grieve my loss of her while she was in fact, losing herself. She had been the first person I would call to boast of some surprising and positive event. No longer could I call to boast or to complain about occurrences in my life. All that was over. I was losing my mother just as she was losing herself. She lost the ability to find words and she loved words. She would begin to speak a thought and stop mid-sentence. Her brain could not track. I would take her for rides in the car and travel the most beautiful roads in Napa and Sonoma Counties. That opportunity faded too, when she could no longer bring her attention much past her nose. She lost the ability to dress herself a long time ago as she became frail, but now she couldn't even assist. She couldn't lift a foot to help me as I tried to put her shoe on. She stood there, while she still could stand, baffled and unable to even begin to maneuver her body to get into the passenger seat of my car. Moment by moment, it became less possible to fathom what it was like to live inside her head. What were her thoughts like? Could she even remember the people she loved? Did she think at all? I tried to bring her hope, though little of it had I.

My mother's parents, Rose and Frank Misino, were married young. My grandmother was 18 when she got married and had my Mom when she was 20. Toni was born in Rochester, New York. When she was very young, she and her family moved to Ninth Avenue and then to Morningside Avenue in Harlem, Manhattan, New York. There was no racism in my grandparents' home. They were newly American and my mother's few friends and classmates came in all colors.

Frank Misino was the neighborhood ice delivery man. He was well liked by everyone and worked hard to support his beautiful wife and young child. He started feeling ill when my mother was two years old, mostly having pain in his legs. Profoundly sad and challenging visits to the doctor revealed, after several years of tests, speculation and incorrect diagnoses, that he was, in fact, suffering from Multiple Sclerosis.

My grandfather, Frank Misino, died when my mother was 17 years old. Of course, I wasn't born yet. My mother talked about him a bit, but times had been hard for her, so hard that she avoided revisiting those years in her life. My grandfather was a really nice man. My mother's friends would visit and sometimes spend the entire visit talking with him. He dissipated as health and capability dripped away from him and pain took their place. There was not much

35

medical help possible at that time. He first walked with a limp, and then a cane, following that with crutches until he could not stand at all. Pictures of him in his "later" years showed a face sculpted by pain and a body withered and riddled with disease.

My grandmother, Rose Misino, went to work to support the family. She did not yet speak English, although she learned quickly because of her inner strength and acute survival instincts. She had been raised in Bisceglie, Italy. It is located, as my mother used to say, "near the heel." My grandmother was born in 1905 when Bisceglie was a small city. Her father made leather products, tack for horses and wagons, etc. Her father was a selfish man, a total womanizer and a wife beater. My great grandmother's life, I was told, was torture. She had ten pregnancies and eight live births. My grandmother, Rose, was the oldest. She was charged with raising her younger siblings, when she wasn't in school or going to the convent to learn how to sew from the nuns. And sew she could! She could have made an entire wedding gown by hand, or tailor a suit for a man. She embroidered perfectly and had absolutely mastered the arts of needle and thread. So it was that she went to work in a factory that made women's gowns for high-end stores such as *Lord & Taylor* and ended up as the overseer who fixed everyone else's mistakes.

While my grandmother was working, my mother had to take care of the duties of the house. She cleaned and washed clothes and even cooked, spaghetti of course, starting at the age of 5. Her father helped where he could, supervising when that was all he had to give.

My grandmother, it might be said, had a cruel side. Perhaps her ability to relate was so far entombed within her from watching her mother get beaten up over and over again. Being helpless to do anything about it, she would not allow herself to connect or trust. She wanted to have a baby boy so much, that she cried when my mother was born. And she told my mother this when my mother was about eight years old. Because of the M.S., because of the financial problems brought on by the depression, as well as the cost of medical care, and as ultimately, my grandfather's body ceased to function, my mother was the only child they had.

My mother recalled incidents where Rose had delivered an undeserved slap across her face for trying to defend her against a spiteful, opinionated assault from a jealous friend. Rose Misino was an unusually pretty woman with delicate features, but inside was constantly on guard and ready to fight to the emotional death anyone who didn't agree with her, except that one obnoxious friend whom she revered. Nothing that friend could do was wrong in Rose's eyes. But if you erred or failed in my grandmother's judgment, her glare was poison enough. She was also quite adept at vicious ridicule. Rose Misino had her own very distinct paradigm. There was no point in explaining anything to her. She saw what she saw, knew what she knew, and ultimately, you deserved what you got. "*Forgot, mistake, I don't know, you didn't tell me,*" was condescendingly chanted to her daughter and to her grandchildren when we'd made a mistake. While Rose Misino did seem merciless, she was fiercely loyal to family, which quality, I suppose, made her believe it was her right to belittle.

Toni DeLuca grew up taking careful, well thought-out steps, steps designed to avoid conflict, catastrophe, or the wrath of her mother. Penmanship was well practiced in those days, and my mother's was perfect, as she was the first to point out.

My Mom and Dad met at New York University. They were both members of the Italian Club. They both loved opera and my mother doted on my father because of his many talents. Peter played mandolin and sang. He tried his hand at opera, but had all passion and no training. His sister, my Aunt Phyllis, was trained and sang really well, I am told. She performed at various times and places and would have shined in her performance on the Ted Mack Amateur hour, had her television appearance

38

Dad left for Syracuse, New York, applying for a job, which he ultimately got. He was turning over a new leaf in life. I think he blamed himself for my mother's affair, her subsequent pregnancy and birth of the little boy he accepted as his own, and for being inadequate. His mental disease was quelled at times, but erupted at others. I found letters from my Dad among my mother's things. He wrote to her complaining of the boredom of his life living in a downtown Syracuse hotel and going to work and having no money for any "fun." It must have galled my mother tremendously as being stuck in this apartment providing constant care to four small ones was not exactly "fun." He sent money, but it was barely enough.

One day, during a short visit from my Dad, he announced that he would take one of us with him to Syracuse for a couple of weeks. He and my Mom must have discussed it ahead of time and although the three of us were raising our hands, and jumping up and down yelling, "take me! take me!" it had already been decided that I, 6-year old Michèle, had been chosen.

The name "Syracuse" landed oddly on my ears. In my very young mind, I pictured a desolated gas station in the middle of the night. Inwardly, I questioned whether I really wanted to go, but I was going with my Daddy and I believed we would be spending a lot of time together, and what could be better than

43

that! Instead, he planted me at Mrs. Miller's, where I stayed
24-hours a day. She had a little dog that wanted nothing to do
with me, and I had nothing to do, no toys, no books, no TV,
nothing for the two weeks I stayed with her. I remember going
with her and waiting for her at the salon while she got her hair
done. She was an older widow with white hair, and the salon had
dyed it blue. Blue hair. She asked me how it looked. It looked
pitiful, but I lied. She was a blue-haired old lady. We had no
rapport at all, and asking me about her hair was just about the
only time she bothered to speak to me in the couple of weeks
I was there. I was alone again, in a sort of solitary confinement
reminiscent of what I had experienced in the foster home, once
again not knowing the planned length of my commitment.

Dad and I had ridden a bus up from New York to Syracuse.
We sang softly songs like, "Down in the station early in the
morning, see the little Pufferbellies all in a row," (written by
Paul Mills and Slim Gaillard). We were close. The bus ride
took 6 hours so for the 6 hours and then some I got to be
with my Dad. Then we ended up at Mrs. Miller's and I saw
him two weeks later when he came to get me to put me on a
plane to go back to New York.

It didn't take long before we all headed to Syracuse,
moving into a lovely three-bedroom apartment which was

the second floor of a house on Court Street. We went to Pere Lemoyne School. We three kids were well-planted there, and yet we would walk home from school arm in arm chanting "*I want to go back to New York. I want to go back to New York.*" If memory serves me, Greg led the chant, but it wasn't really New York we all wanted to return to. It was the life we had on MacDougal Street. It was the life untarnished by foster homes, head lice, grief, separation from one another and loneliness. It was the child's life when a skinned knee was the worst experience we could possibly know. It was Childhood. Unblemished Childhood.

There were aspects of Syracuse life that we loved. Snow. Schiller Park and sledding. Long drives with Dad and Mom (now pregnant again) and Baby Stevie in the front seat and the three older kids huddled in the back seat for warmth. We always stopped at a particular drive-thru for hamburgers and shakes. The shakes, which lasted longer than the hamburgers, were freezing, and as we froze ourselves from the inside out from what was already a chilly car in a Northeastern winter, we huddled closer and closer to each other. It was ecstasy.

It was the beginning of Spring now. The soft golden sunlight warmed the cold winter air with only a promise, a promise which felt so incredibly good. We came home from school that Wednesday afternoon and played outside the house. Mom was in the hospital. Her baby had died, and just as the little baby boy she was pregnant with after having me did, this infant girl got to experience only a few moments of breath before she returned to that Nothing she came from. I don't remember feeling sad. Everything just felt surreal, alien. Mommy was in the hospital and we waited for Daddy to return from work, feed us his version of dinner, and then we would go to bed to wake up to Daddy's form of us getting ready for school. Strange. It was Monday, April 17th when the baby died and my mother remained in the hospital. The prediction was that she would remain there for about a week. This was just Wednesday. The week already seemed to go on forever.

My father's days must have been really challenging. We were good kids and did what we could. We would get our own breakfast, likely cheerios or maybe cocoa puffs. All healthy food rules were suspended until the return of our Mom. We would all leave the house at the same time. Greg, Dorie and I would walk the two blocks to school. Dad would take Baby Stevie to the babysitter, a co-worker's wife who had generously offered to pitch in at this awful time. Then he would go off to work. I suppose that on that wretched Monday when the baby died, he must have spent a good deal of time at the hospital where my mother, after full labor, delivered a swollen, blue

46

lump of a baby girl that she knew, during the full course of her pregnancy and from past experience, was not to survive. I wonder if they cried together. I wonder if they were truthful and told each other that their tears were a goulash of grief, relief and guilt. Or did they cry together in silence, unable to reveal, even to themselves, the sacrilege of their conflicted emotions? Thus far it seemed that life had schooled them in cruelty. Four children who personified love and joy and gifted them with a purpose for life, a purpose whose threshold they could barely reach. One more would have tilted the scales and we would all cascade down into an unspeakable abyss. So there was relief. And there was undoubtedly guilt.

Now it was Wednesday, and while we never spoke of our sense of how unstable seemed our circumstance, we played. As the sun began to set, we began to wonder where our father was. The winter reminded us that it had not yet left us and our fingers and toes grew cold with its uncaring touch. It was getting dark and Daddy was not yet home.

None of us had a key to the apartment and just as the cold began to be unbearable, our father's friend and co-worker drove up. He asked us to get in his car and told us that our father wanted us to come with him for dinner. Well-schooled not to go with anyone ever, we huddled and discussed it. Greg decided it would be okay to go. This was Daddy's friend. We climbed into the car and headed off for dinner. We were kids, giggling and sharing kid-talk together as three close siblings are apt to do, and it must have been torture for my father's friend and his wife, knowing what we did not yet know.

We were driven home and ran to our Mom who sat on the couch in the living room. There was also a priest and a couple of other men there. None of them was my Dad. I can see my Mom in my mind's eye bracing herself when one of my father's friends looked out the window at our arrival and called out, "they're here." How does one face a moment like this?

We hugged and kissed our Mom; we had all missed her so very much. The three of us huddled as the priest began to speak.

"You know Jesus is in Heaven, don't you?"

"Yes," we answered simultaneously.

"Well, when God wanted Jesus back in Heaven, he called him back. And Jesus went to be with him. When God needed Joseph in Heaven, he called to him, and Joseph went. And the same with Mother Mary. When God needed Mary in Heaven, he

called to her, and Mary went. And now God needs your Father in Heaven, and that is where he is."

Tears were silently falling down my mother's face. Greg began to softly sob and Dorie followed. I, being just seven, didn't fully understand, but the sight of my mother and my brother and sister as they sobbed quietly, soon to have their sobs become full-on wails, tore at my heart and soul. Their crying got louder and louder. I did not fully comprehend that I would never see my Daddy again, but the depth of despair shared by my mother and my siblings was not lost on me. I was afraid, desperately sad, and thoroughly confused. I knew, somehow, that life would never be the same again.

Peter DeLuca had had a couple of heart attacks before the one that extinguished his life. He was at work when he felt the pressure in his chest begin to grow, so he asked his friend to drive him to the doctor. Halfway there, he told his friend that this pain felt much worse than any chest pain he'd felt before. He asked his friend to please take him to the hospital. They stopped at the red light on the corner of the hospital, where my Dad breathed his last breath. His friend has had to live with that. There is no way of knowing that had they reached the hospital, had they aimed for the hospital in the first place, had they arrived with minutes to spare, if Peter DeLuca could have lived. And had he lived, how long, how well would he have lived? Unanswerable questions have always invaded my peace of mind like chiding ghosts one can never escape.

8

Brooklyn

My grandmother came up to Syracuse to help. We packed up what we could and ended up in Brooklyn in her tiny apartment on Rogers Avenue. Steve and I slept on piles of blankets on the floor. There was a double bed in the bedroom and a cot somewhere. I don't remember where everyone else slept. I suppose my grandmother slept in her bed and probably shared it with my mother, who was well trained since childhood that her mother would not tolerate any movement in the middle of the night. Change your position and you would be rudely awakened by an irritated smack.

Greg and Dorie went to the public school a few blocks away, and somehow, once again I was told how fortunate I was. I was enrolled into St. Jerome's Catholic School. My parents had been married in that church, and now I was to complete 2nd grade there.

Fortunate I was, ecstatically fortunate, because my teacher was Sr. Mary Jogues, the kindest person I have ever met. The other children in the class felt the same way, and on my first day, I was unprepared for milk and cookie time. Sr. Mary Jogues managed a milk for me and then told the other pupils that I, the new girl, didn't know about milk and cookie time. "Is there anyone who would like to share their cookies with Michèle?" There was not a child in the class who didn't rush over to add to the mountain of donated cookies. I felt totally welcomed and honored, although I knew then as I know now that their generosity was their jumping for joy for any opportunity to please our beloved Sr. Mary Jogues.

Second grade went quickly, as I had entered the school in May and the school semester ended the last day of June.

In the summer, we moved to a huge housing complex. Each building had six floors with six apartments each. Our block alone could boast of 16 of these buildings, and there were several blocks more equally populated with such buildings. They were called "The Vanderveer Estates." Barbra Streisand grew up there, and being a few years older than me, babysat some of my classmates. I never did meet her, but as she climbed in her fame, many neighbors boasted that they had known her and had watched her grow up.

There was a large courtyard in the center of the block surrounded by all of these buildings. Every day we could safely go out to play, finding children in our age group playing ball or jumping rope. There was never a scarcity of children, and despite my terrible shyness, I made a friend or two and I was happy.

Third grade found me in Sr. Mary Evangela's class. She was a tiny, pretty nun, who spewed sarcasm at every opportunity. She was mean to the boys, particularly, dragging them up to the front of the room by the ear for offenses such as talking in class. Knuckles were rapped with rulers and boys struggled not to be betrayed by their own tears.

It was to be our first Christmas without our Dad. My Grandmother provided us with a small artificial tree and way too many baubles and balls to weigh its branches down. I just had my 8th birthday, and I sported a gap in my front teeth to prove it.

My mother sat us down, Gregory, Dorie and me, to explain how little money she had. She said she could buy us presents or we could have a nice dinner together. One or the other. Well, I guess now there could be no more pretending that I believed in Santa Claus. We agreed on the nice dinner only because my mother had slanted her proposal for that response. None of us wanted to disappoint her, yet in our heart of hearts, had we been honest, we wanted Christmas presents. What child wouldn't!

I could not believe there would be no Christmas presents. I barely slept. No Christmas presents! Really? Impossible! I finally fell asleep just before it got light and woke up to my sister and older brother excitedly running to the living room to look under the tree, even though we all knew for sure there would be no presents for us. Yet hope abided. My mother had bought and wrapped two little cars for Steve, who was nearly two, but nothing for the older children. Suddenly, Dorie and I noticed two small identical packages, one marked for her and one marked for me. Greg had bought us gifts. Greg had bought each of us a watercolor set that cost 5 cents at the "Five and Ten" around the corner. They were small gifts for each of us, but big relief that we had *something* under the tree. I was sad for Greg, who received nothing, and I was thankful then as I am thankful now at what a kind and considerate big brother he can be!

Third grade ended that next year in June and another eternal summer began. There was a playground right across the street, abutting our school. Dorie and I loved the swings and we would take our little brother there and put him on the "baby" swings.

We would ride the "see-saw" and Greg would play ball. The forever of summer would finally end with the excitement of a new school year. My Mom bought us each a new pair of sneakers at the beginning of the summer and now she bought us each a new pair of shoes for school. We got Bic pens, pencils and notebooks and loose leaf paper. It was all pretty simple stuff, not the glittery, fancy stuff of today. Still, the newness of it all filled us with an enthralling anticipation as we began our new school year. I had a new class in public school, new pupils and a new teacher, Mrs. Auerbach. My sister had been her pupil two years before. I, a tiny child, shy and emotionally battered by what my life had been up to then, was an easy target. Mrs. Auerbach ruthlessly belittled me day after day, tearing up my papers, ridiculing me, and yelling in my face, spraying me with her spittle and screaming that I was the stupidest child she ever had to teach. The other kids would laugh uncontrollably and all that was left of me was a deep yearning to disappear, evaporate, or fall down a hole never to be seen again. I believed her—she was a teacher, after all, and if she says I am stupid then stupid I must be. I was terrified. What if my mother finds out that I am stupid? Would she return me to the foster home? Or would she just throw me out into the street?

Fern Fleckman lived upstairs in the same apartment line and we were in the same class. We played together during the summer and she would knock on our door to "call for me" so that we could walk to school together. One day, as I finished my lunch and was about to gather my things to return to school, Fern asked my mother, "Mrs. DeLuca, what would you think of a teacher who yells at a pupil all the time, tears up all their papers and yells in their face that they are stupid?" "Oh, that's terrible! Does your teacher do that?" "Yes," responded Fern. "To which child?" Fern turned and looked at me, as did my mother with a look of horror on her face. But the horror was mine, as was the humiliation and the fear that I had been found out. Now my mother knows that I am stupid. What is going to happen?

I remember the heat flushing my face and the sickening feeling in my stomach. How could a teacher be wrong? But my mother assured me she was, and marched up to the school to the principal's office.

It was a story she told over and over again, a story she regarded as her great success, never realizing it had only exacerbated the bleak circumstances of my school life. Her story was, that even though she never raised her voice, she told that weak and worthless principal and Mrs. Auerbach that she would not tolerate her daughter being treated that way. "I was nice to your other daughter," Mrs. Auerbach asserted, thinking that somehow this would make an adequate defense. The principal agreed to remove me from that class and transfer me to Mrs. Ephraim's class, but my mother insisted it be Mrs. Appelbaum's. And so it was.

The fourth grade was divided into four classes: the smartest, two second smartest, and the stupid class. This was the understanding of every fourth grader that year. So while my mother's story made her a hero mostly to herself and, I presume, to any of the neighbors she regularly gossiped with, for me it only proved Mrs. Auerbach's point. I was too stupid for the smartest class. And now every fourth grader knew it.

Mrs. Appelbaum was the stricter of the two teachers for the *second smartest classes*. So my mother had been told. Ultimately, Mrs. Appelbaum was a good teacher, albeit a cruel one. Her cruelty was judiciously handed out to all her students so we simply shared our collective cringes.

Sometime around fifth grade, my brother Greg and I had gotten into some mischief. I loved our camaraderie and our status as co-conspirators. Suffice it to say that he led his sister, four years his junior, into some bad behavior. I never held him accountable for it, instead savoring the delight of our secret conspiracy. Greg, however, must have felt intolerably guilty, and later that day began a comedy routine scapegoat attack at the dinner table, with me, and only me, as the object of his ridicule. I had no ability to defend myself. I remember looking at him, watching him laugh at his own one-liners the point of which was, *I was stupid.* Having been verbally abused by her mother, my mother did nothing to defend me, but instead encouraged Greg. I was not allowed to leave the table and had to endure yet another shaming. There was no escape. The comedy routine and its encouragement lasted for the rest of my years of living at home and then beyond. *I was stupid.* I was *stupid* at home. I was *stupid* at school. There was simply too much evidence for it not to be true. *I was stupid.* Needless to say, I was also miserable and had no fight in me. Even my friend Fern would only be my friend when no one would see. We would walk to the corner and she would cross at the green light, with me, dutifully waiting for the next green light so we would not be seen together by any of our classmates.

My school experience was confusing. I never did homework. Where could I? Our apartment was small, the TV constantly on, entertaining my brother six years my junior. My reading level soared, despite the fact that I had a hard time reading. It was very difficult work. I could read the words, but my brain would not absorb them. I was constantly in trouble for not completing homework.

I took a book out of the library. It was about Abraham Lincoln. I never read it and now a book report was due. So I faked it. *Abraham Lincoln cut down the cherry tree*, but he could not tell a lie. But I could. And boy, was I in trouble!

My mother would continuously chide me about Abraham Lincoln and the cherry tree for years. Neither she nor my teacher questioned why I would do such a thing. No one helped me read the book and rectify my bad actions with a proper book report. It was more proof that I was damaged goods, or worse, like my father, I was born defective.

I would say I was a shadow of myself throughout junior high school, but you have to have a self to cast a shadow. I was a tiny clump of worthlessness trying desperately not to be noticed. I never considered striving. It was not an option to have likes or dislikes or goals. All I wanted to do was disappear.

I began, as most pre-teenagers do, noticing my surroundings. I began noticing the kids who were supposed to have been my peers, but instead appeared to me to range from normal (and perhaps boring) to special, inspired and inspiring. I was merely invisible. After a couple of months of watching the interactions of my schoolmates, I deduced that

59

there were four girls who were popular. I suspect that nearly every other girl in the ninth grade wished to be one of them.

Recognizing that I was utterly irredeemable and could fall no lower than the bottom of my personal hell, I became determined to copy them. Act like them. Dress like them. Talk like them. Laugh like them. I even changed my handwriting to mimic the best of theirs. Naturally, everyone in the class noticed. I had, unbeknownst to me, quite a knack for theater. Since I was bussed in, however, I would carry the dishonor only during school hours. When I returned home to my neighborhood, I continued my theater and found that kids actually liked this newly created "*me.*" Of course, it wasn't *me*, and I found little true redemption in my theatrical performance. If the other kids believed the performance, then something must be wrong with them, too.

Little by little, almost by accident, the real me began to materialize. I began to fight for my identity. Most teenagers do, I think, and many, like me, begin to rebel. I started smoking cigarettes at the age of 14 and blatantly lied when my mother found a half-smoked pack in my jacket pocket. It was an experiment in reality. Reality sucked for me anyway. My mother had betrayed me by supporting my brother's bullying of me. I was giving her what I thought she deserved. Besides, what consequences could compete with being the lowest of the low? What could possibly befall someone who had no value whatsoever?

My grandmother was so angered at this behavior of mine which she simply could not comprehend. She stopped speaking to me entirely, and although she would go home to her tiny apartment every night, only a ten-minute walk away, she spent daytimes at our apartment. No one but no one could survive my grandmother's hateful glare. I could no longer come home after school, but had to find places to bide my time until my mother would come home after work. So I, as they say, "ran the streets."

9

Elephant Bells

Fourteen years old. I couldn't wait to get started. Life. My life. A date with a boy. A cute boy. A self-righteous, obnoxious 17-year-old boy doused in Jade East. A total juvenile delinquent type—like West Side Story. A Puerto Rican, but he looked like Riff. A Jet and a Shark all put together, and put together well, at that. His shirts were always pressed. For that matter, so were his pants. He didn't have a big wardrobe, but his clothes were always clean and crisp. Fourteen years old. Yup. I was smitten.

My eyes were big and I flirted with them easily. I was delighted that Bobby had noticed me. How could he not? Neon flashing signs and little girl sighs in his presence. He noticed. As well he noticed that I would be easy to manipulate, probably easy in general.

How many times had I whined at him, "I wanna go dancing." Not that I knew how to dance. I was skinny, my body even younger in some ways than my fourteen years. I was knobby-kneed, had pointy-elbows and I moved those legs and arms like they were just recently borrowed. Even worse, if you were looking, you would think I was dancing to totally different music. I could not find the beat. My face would flush red and those big brown eyeballs would dart around their white pools, eyes open wide out of abject fear, as I tried to avoid anyone's eye contact. I kept hoping I wasn't seen. I kept hoping to be invisible. And still, I whined, "Bobby, when are you going to take me dancing?" "I wanna go dancing." "When are you going to take me?"

"You wouldn't want me to take you dancing," Bobby asserted. "I like to dance with all the girls. Not just one. You wouldn't be happy." "I don't care! I wanna go dancing!" (*Liar! Liar! Liar!*) I wanted a first date. I wanted Bobby to take me dancing and never leave my side. But let's just start by giving me my way. Eventually, Bobby did.

"Okay," he said. "We will go Saturday. But you're not going to like it. I like to dance with all the girls! Pick you up at 7."

We were going to a place that served no alcohol and where a DJ played records, a place where fourteen-year-olds and seventeen-year-olds could go. The Hullaballoo. What a thrill! My first date! And with the perfect boy! One who was unavailable, unattainable, rude and self-interested, one who overflowed with conceit. A perfect date for a fourteen-year-old girl with no confidence trying to prove to herself she was okay, but knowing in her heart of hearts that she was defective. Unfixable. Unlovable and unworthy. Yes, Bobby was perfect.

Saturday morning when I awoke, I had more energy than I knew what to do with. I had always been like that. The excitement and anticipation made an hour seem like a week and a minute seem to not move at all. I could barely breathe! I was going dancing. And with Bobby.

Realizing that I had nothing to wear that would be right for this very special first date, I grabbed the few dollars from my piggy bank and walked around the corner to Nostrand Avenue. I passed the famous Ebingers; you know, the bakery famous for their "black-out cakes" and I passed National Shoes and a few other stores and went right into the Five and Ten. That's what we called it. It wasn't Woolworth's, but it well could have been. Lots of little things, inexpensive and cheap, but for me, at fourteen, with just the money from my piggy bank, it was perfect.

I found the remnants table and looked through, and after deliberating upon each and every piece of cloth, settled for an off-white with avocado green threads running horizontally and vertically, creating a kind of a woven look, a soft plaid. It would not have been my choice at all, but my choices were so limited. And since I was possessed of some creative urge and limited by time, the fabric chose me.

I looked through the Simplicity patterns. "Ah, here's one," I thought. Back in the late sixties, a one-piece sort of jumpsuit became fashionable. They called it loungewear and the pattern I chose was such, two pattern pieces for the front and two pattern pieces for the back. The front halter top was one piece with its lower counterpart, but I chose to cut the top off. I sewed and sewed, even using my grandmother's sewing machine which could have landed me in some serious trouble had something gone wrong. I did not really know how to use it, but either desperation or creativity led me and before I knew it, I had these beautiful flowing "elephant bells." Elephant bell bottom pants did not come into style for another year, but there they were. Precocious as sometimes I could be, precocious inside of my soup of naïveté, self-loathing and fear, I designed something especially fashionable just before they came into fashion. There was something courageous in me, some huge and relentless appetite. I wanted a life. I wanted a normal life. And I wanted to go dancing and I wanted something nice to wear. Now I had elephant bells and I was going to go dancing with Bobby and I wanted it to be magical. In a totally unexpected way, magical it was.

Bobby arrived on time and I was ready, perfect hair, white lacy blouse which was a hand-me-down from my big sister and really didn't fit me right, and, of course, my new pants. Nervousness painted my entire face bright pink and I tried to act as if going dancing, *going dancing with Bobby*, of all people, was normal. I tried to pretend I was normal. Well, normal it might have been for some *normal* girl. But I knew the *truth*, that I was not normal and that I had better fake it and fake it well.

First we went to Jahn's on Flatbush Avenue. Jahn's was famous for their ice cream creations. I was shy and scared of the prospect of eating in front of Bobby. We looked at our menus and decided. The waitress came over and Bobby ordered, "Banana split with strawberry and chocolate ice cream and a chocolate shake." The waitress wrote the order on her small pad and turned to walk away. "Wait!" Bobby said, pointing to me. "She didn't order." I ordered chocolate ice cream with whipped cream. We ate and left for the dance.

We entered the Hullaballoo and my skin crawled with both fear and excitement. My face flushed and every move I made seemed robotic and awkward. Bobby saw two of his friends and left me standing there while he went to say hello. All of a sudden six girls surrounded me and said "hi." "Hi," I responded, praying that my defectiveness would not be noticed. "*Where* did you get those pants?" one of them asked. And there I was, enveloped in my shyness, driven by some inner need to be fully alive, unsure of every step, every movement and unsure of anything I would say, I heard myself say, "I made them." Yes, proudly I said it. "I made them." My declaration of worthiness; no, even more. My declaration of ascension to the top of the moment. I aced it. I made those pants!

Bobby came over and brought his two friends with him. Boo was a physically solid guy, probably destined for some blue-collar construction work, a physically fit "bear" of a boy. Danny, was taller, thinner, loose of limb, with a gentle, sweet face. Bobby walked away and Boo and Danny began to take turns dancing with me. They had play arguments. "No. She said she would dance the next slow one with me!" "Well, maybe, but she said she would dance the next dance with me! You had your turn!" And then they turned to me and asked me to choose.

What a magical first date. How these two boys both championed me and made this an evening I would remember for the rest of my life! For the first time in my life, I was a princess!

But all this magic didn't dispel the symptoms of my inner dis-ease, my need to stay in my world, to be treated as if I were worthless, broken, spiritually deformed.

Boo and Danny asked me to wait; they'd be right back. Apparently, they walked over to Bobby and announced that they would take me home. Bobby came back angry as hell at their proposition, and even though I had not even danced with him once, I left with him.

In my heart of hearts, forevermore, I am grateful for my first date, my first dances with those two kind and generous gentlemen of perhaps sixteen and seventeen years old. So thank you, Boo, and thank you, Danny. Wherever you are. For seeing in me what I could not see in myself for many years to come and for treating me like a lady, thank you.

And I plead, as well, for my own forgiveness. So accustomed was I to those people who supposedly "loved me" wearing down any inkling of self-esteem and proving to me over and over again that I was worthless! I didn't talk right, walk right, my ideas were stupid, and I was a waste of human breath. I left with Bobby, accompanied by that "not enough" feeling, that sense that my soul was bleeding and that there was no love and acceptance that could ever fill the empty vessel that I was. My heart swelled with that familiar emptiness, just as the bellies of starving children swell as the rest of them dissipates and fades. My soul so empty that all my inner conversations of worthlessness echoed over their canyons, and I was at home.

10

Frankie Russo

There has never been such a beautiful boy. He was Perfect! And there he was, flirting with me. M*e!!!* He was on the corner of Flatbush and Newkirk in Brooklyn, a corner where a group of teenagers hung out. I was 15. Frankie was 16. He asked me if I wanted to jump on his bike so he could give me a ride. We tried, but it didn't work. The handlebars cut into my bum and were painful, and he was, I'd realize weeks later, too high to manage a bicycle. It was February 7th, 1969. I remember because exactly a week later, on Valentine's Day, he asked me to go steady. "Do you really want me to?" I asked, totally flustered. "No," he responded with pure Brooklyn sarcasm. "Why do you think I asked?" Of course I said yes, nearly pinching myself in disbelief that such a beautiful, beautiful boy would want me.

Frankie was a nice guy, although I had heard how he would beat the crap out of his previous girlfriend. He only hit me once, and once was more than enough, and that was on the day I broke up with him for good. He gave me one good hard slap across my face. My nose bled and my lip immediately swelled. Breaking up with him was one of the hardest things I ever did. Frankie was my first love and truly, he was beautiful inside and out. By the time I met him, he had developed quite a serious heroin habit. The two years we were together were fraught with the kinds of challenges a young heroin addict would face. Those challenges sullied my life as well.

The regularly-occurring problem was that he would be very late in picking me up, and sometimes he wouldn't at all. We would talk on the phone just before he would leave his house. He lived on Hicks Street, supposedly Brooklyn Heights, but the tiny apartment that he, his parents and his brother lived in overlooked the highway, was historically old, in disrepair, loud, and he was very much ashamed of it. He'd have to take the subway to my apartment, and usually, if he didn't stop to pick up his drug, the trip would take about 45 minutes. He'd never tell me of his intentions to "cop" (buy) heroin before he was to show up, and often he was waylaid by not having enough cash, not finding his dealer home, or not finding a place to shoot up. Years later I realized that the hysteria I felt when he didn't show up on time had an original source. That sick feeling lasted until I could finally cast eyes

upon him and arms around him. It reminded me of the day
I waited in vain for my father to show up at the foster home.
No matter how many times Frank was late, each time I felt
like I was going to die.

When he was16 year old, he was arrested for possession
of heroin and his syringe (he'd refer to them as his "works"),
I spent my days in hysteria waiting for him to return, as he
spent his days in Riker's Island jail.

I had been so deeply influenced by West Side Story that
I wanted to be his *Maria*. I thought that if I believed in him
enough, if I loved him enough, he would turn his life around.
But how? I had no idea how to navigate life. He had dropped
out, while I continued the farce they called high school. He
had, at one point, a part-time job engraving trophies.

My clothes were all hand-me-downs, and while some of
the dresses I had worn to school were quite nice, I was now
wearing "seafarer" jeans that were way too long. The bottoms
dragged along the ground and were always ripped and dirty.
Frankie, however, was always immaculate. As children, my
siblings and I generally bathed only a few times a year, for
special occasions such as Easter or Christmas or the first day
of school. Now, because of Frankie's influence, I showered

73

every day, but my clothes were the same old, funky ones I usually wore to hang out.

When Frankie received his first paycheck from his trophy engraving job, he took me to Sears on Flatbush Avenue. It was both humiliating and exciting as he grabbed blouses off the rack chiding me, "what's wrong with this one? And this one? What's wrong with this one?" He spent his entire first paycheck on me and I am still moved to tears when I think of that day.

Frankie's mother would be picked up by his father in his father's taxi cab at 10:00 p.m. each night and be driven to work where she cleaned office buildings. Frankie and I would watch from down the block as the cab drove away and then we would climb the spiral brick stairs to his apartment. Ashamed of that apartment as he was, he lied to me the very first time we went there to have sex. He told me it was his friend's. But soon he confessed that it was where he lived. It didn't matter to me. My apartment did not seem much better.

Mostly, we hung out with a bunch of us hippie kids on the corner of Flatbush and Newkirk in Brooklyn. There were different locations where teenagers would gather. There were the "acid freaks," the "downers," the "speed freaks" and the "hitters." Flatbush and Newark kids were downers and hitters, mostly. Some were addicted to heroin, as was Frankie. Some liked to take downers, such as tuminols and seconals. Some liked to fight. We all smoked pot. We told stories and laughed, talked about Led Zeppelin, the Rolling Stones, the Beatles and others. Sometimes we'd find our way to an apartment when parents were out. Mostly, we were just troubled kids seeking comfort in each other's company and pretending to belong when there was really nothing to belong to.

On occasion, Frankie and I had a real date. We went to some movie in one of Flatbush Avenue's most plush movie theaters. The theater was full, so it must have been a new release. We sat up in the balcony, generally engrossed in what was on the screen. I had learned a lot from Frankie who had nearly a fetish for cleanliness. I had not been reared to shower regularly and as kids in my family, the order to "go brush your teeth" was generally ignored. But now I had a boyfriend, and we would make out. We both smoked cigarettes (I changed to his brand to prove my love for him) and I am sure the fetid stench of both our mouths covered up any other odor. Now, in order to be right for Frankie, I showered daily, washed and blow-dried my hair daily and even brushed my teeth.

Frankie's hair was always perfect, and his clothes were always neat and clean. He kept a comb in his back pocket to ensure his hair was always at its best. So there we were, sitting in the full balcony of the movie theater, watching the movie as we should. The seats were plush velvet red and were rimmed in some dark tarnished metal. Frankie had his arm around me with his hand just about resting on that metal rim of my seat. Comb in hand, he started his nervous habit of tapping the comb on that metal rim, just inches from my ear. "Frankie, stop it," I whispered. He did, only to unconsciously start again. "*Frankie, stop it!*" I reiterated, slightly more emphatically, but still in a whisper. Moments later he started yet again, this time, the tapping inspired such frustration in me that I demanded, loudly, not realizing how loud I was, "Frankie, *STOP IT!*" The entire balcony and some of the mezzanine broke into applause. "Yay Frankie! You go, Frankie!!!"

Frankie was my first love and I still remember the feel of him, the smell of him, as it seemed we were magnetically drawn to always be in each other's embrace.

It was on December 17th, 1970. My 16th birthday was December 18th, and I had great expectations as to how magical being sweet sixteen would be. Frankie, as he usually did, arrived late. He had gone to "cop" his heroin. He arrived at my house with face flushed and in a sweat. We went into my room and he told me that he had gone to Willie's, his drug dealer. But

Willie wasn't home. As he came down the hallway stairs he saw a man standing beneath the stairwell. He recognized the man as the beat cop, now dressed in civilian clothes. Frankie ran, and despite his abuse of his body with heroin, cigarettes and pot, his track running talent had not left him. He had his works in his pocket and was afraid of being arrested again. He ran; the cop ran after him. When he didn't stop, the cop shot his gun at him and thankfully missed.

These were the travails of being the girlfriend of a junkie. There had been another time when we were in a car with his friend, Donny. We stopped at a building. Donny went into cop drugs. As Donny got back into the car, a gun was suddenly pointed at his head by a plain-clothed policeman. Donny was just 17. I don't know how Donny managed to hide the tiny bag of heroin he just scored, but he did. Answering the cop with a "yes, sir" or a "no sir," we escaped discovery and were able to drive away. I was scared, and although Donny had been in fear for his life with a gun pointed at his head, he still managed not to betray himself.

On December 17th, we stayed in. It had snowed and it was cold outside. Certainly none of our teenage friends would be hanging out on the corner at Flatbush and Newkirk. My ten-year-old brother was in his underwear as my entire family sat in the living room and watched TV together. Our reusable fake Christmas tree was once again over-bedazzled as its gaudy colors and multi-colored lights flickered and lit the room. At midnight, now the first minutes of my 16th birthday, everyone wished me a happy birthday, as I sat on Frankie's lap. How exciting it was, I thought, to finally be 16. Sweet Sixteen! I was sure it was going to be magical. It turned out to be the opposite.

At about 20 minutes after midnight the phone rang. The phone *never* rang at such a late hour in my house. My Mom answered and I could tell listening to just her side of the conversation that something was gravely wrong. I begged Frankie to leave, but he didn't. He wouldn't. Ten minutes later the doorbell rang. My mother answered it. Ten cops and a couple of detectives marched in, some with their guns drawn and aimed at Frankie. I was dragged away from him by a cop and blocked from coming anywhere near him. He was handcuffed and told he was being arrested for *attempted murder of a police officer.*

It was impossible. I knew it. I had been all over Frankie, always, not only all over his body but all over his life. Frankie never had a gun. The cop lied. I believed then as I do now that the cop lied because he had to explain why he discharged his gun on a Brooklyn street. He had to explain why he endangered the public. He had to explain why he shot at a 17-year-old who was running away.

My mother and I joined his mother as she bailed him out of Riker's Island jail. She surrendered her bankbook to the bondsman, and I am sure that must have been her life savings. She was a cleaning woman; her husband was a cab driver who had not only supported Frank and his two siblings as they grew up, but also his first family of several children. That savings account was filled with hard work and sacrifice. I went with her when she met with a lawyer whom she had to pay a $1,000 retainer, a small fortune at that time, especially for someone who had sacrificed so much to save it.

A couple of months between this incident and the trial, I found myself standing in front of that beat cop who walked up to a small group of us teenagers as we hung out in front of the pizza place. He said he planned to testify that he never saw the flash of the gun. Was it conscience that had that slime bag cop change his story or just the flimsiness of his case? Thankfully, he had thought up a way to dispel the misery he had created and rectify the grievous travesty beset upon this 17-year-old innocent minor. The nightmare would soon be over, leaving scars on the soul of Frankie and on the souls of all those who loved him and believed him. That cop's actions had caused the depletion of his parents' meager hard-earned savings. I hope, with all the hope in my heart, that should that cop still be alive, he was and always will be haunted by the detriment he caused so many people with his cowardly lies.

At some point during my 17th year, when Frank and I had been together just over two years, I realized that he was not going to heal. There was little hope for Frank to become anything other than a heroin addict. There was no help from grown-ups, and he was lost in his addiction. His older sister, Carole, tried to talk to him. She told him about a girl who was so beautiful and popular that Carole wanted to *be* her, change identities. Carole's self-esteem had been so low, she would have traded lives with *anyone*, if she could have. I sat and listened and saw myself in her story. This perfect girl who earned Carole's admiration, it turns out, had died from cancer before she was 20 years old. Carole told Frankie that being alive is not a given and that we must make the most of who we are and what we have NOW. She tried to find out why Frank seemed to have such low self-esteem, but Frank would not answer her questions. Frank did not know.

Sitting on the steps in the hallway on the fifth floor where I lived, and reckoning that I, like Frank, would never progress if nothing changed, I broke up with Frankie. At first he didn't believe me, as we had broken up several times before until my yearning for him, my addiction for him broke me down and we'd get back together. But this time it was different. I had to convince him, convince myself that it *had* to be over. So I lied. "I don't love you anymore," I declared. He hauled off and smacked me, causing my bloody nose and swollen lip. My mother heard me cry out and came out of our apartment to rescue me and send him away.

Years later he asked his sister, Carole, who had become a dear friend, for my phone number. He called me, wanting to come to California where I now live. We were in our late 30s and I knew from his sister that his heroin addiction had transformed to an alcohol addiction. I knew he was again violent in his relationships. I realized that we would never again be the good things we had been as a young couple. It was too late for us. I told him how much I wished that some adult somewhere had noticed our struggles, as individuals and as a couple, and helped us. Had we grown up in a small town, into healthy families instead of the ones we each had which were rife with problems, perhaps we would have been married and had a couple of kids together. Perhaps we would have grown old together. But we didn't. That was just a fantasy.

11

Carole

Frank just stared off into space as she spoke. She kept asking him, "what's the matter? What is bothering you?" He wouldn't answer. Perhaps he couldn't answer. Why was he trashing his life? She did all she could to inspire him, give him hope. He was impenetrable, as if he was holding the world's biggest secret. In his sixteen-year-old mind, it must have seemed the world would cease to be if he were to divulge the source of his pain. It seemed he would take that secret to his grave and that secret would be his tombstone. I, on the other hand, felt my heart flutter with the generosity of her words. I knew I was selling myself way short by being with him and following his lead. He was beautiful to my eye, and mores to my heart, such that even the tarnish of his heroin habit and everything ugly that came with it couldn't dim my love for him.

I watched Carole and the natural grace she had despite her exasperation. I listened to each pleading word and hoped he would hear what I heard. She was blonder than Frank, whose hair color would change from light brown to blonde, depending upon the season. I was nine years her junior and she was an angel. She was the only one who had spoken the truth, who acknowledged this torn-up path he followed, and had shown any faith in him besides me. Authentic words poured out of her. Everything she did or said seemed heartfelt and I was in awe.

We visited her apartment and her family, which consisted of her dark-skinned Puerto Rican husband, a 5-year-old boy and a 2-year-old girl, both brown with large dark eyes. It was shocking to see a mixed family in 1969 because it was so rare, and here she was, big beautiful blue eyes and blonde hair, she so obviously contrasted her husband. Carole epitomized courage and authenticity. She loved her children and never spoke down to them in any way. No silly little voices. She was direct. I watched as other children who came to visit her kids would chose instead to converse with Carole as she asked them about their lives. They would open the doors of their young hearts to her and tell her their life stories, brief as they were, and yet deeply meaningful to them. They told her their secrets, spoke not only about what they loved and what they had experienced, but also about what they hoped for and what they feared. How was it that Frank could not be moved by her?

I continued to visit her after Frank and I broke up and she became the first real friend of my choosing in what was, at this point, my 17-year-old existence. She began to confide in me her struggles in her marriage. I watched helplessly once or twice when her husband backhanded her for speaking her mind. She was hurt, yes, and she was deeply embarrassed. He began to beat her up more often and when the police were called they separated the couple until at last, her husband had calmed down and then they let him back in the apartment. Finally, she filed for a restraining order and for a divorce, but he kept returning and if he caught her outside her apartment door, she paid dearly. Cops were called but once again, they would calm him down and refuse to arrest him or make him leave. She lived in the Projects, on the second floor, just above the sturdy awning above the entrance door and just below her kitchen window. The apartment doors were metal, well-bolted and impenetrable. Thankfully. Her kitchen window, adjacent to that awning had security bars. We were in the apartment one evening; a few other young people and I were there when he came banging and kicking on the door. She would not let him in. He continued to bang and kick as she yelled for him to go away. "It's over," she yelled. Then he stopped and we breathed a sigh of relief only to find that moments later, he had climbed onto that awning and onto the kitchen window ledge, screaming in fury and trying to pull those security bars off the window. He wasn't able to, and the police finally came and this time, made him leave. I think had he been able to break his way into the apartment, she would have been dead.

Little by little as her life changed, so did mine. On rare occasions she would be able to find a babysitter and we would go to Greenwich Village, share in an exotic Indian meal or watch some folk singers or poets on a dusty old stage. I was proud to know her and we stayed friends through two more husbands. Her authenticity with me dripped away a little at a time. She soon wanted to make no effort to support the friendship. I could visit, but since she developed a dislike for driving, I would have to take a long subway trip and even longer bus ride to see her. She became distant on our coast-to-coast telephone calls and mocked gifts I had sent her. She declared us too different and after numerous tries on my part to express that my love and respect had not changed, she opted out. It took me a long while to accept that because I hate to give up on people. Ultimately, I had no choice.

12

The Rapes

They were called "buffalo sandals." I don't know why. They were made of a neutral leather criss-cross over the front of the foot and a strap across the ankle. In 1974, they were also platformed. I had a job interview and I borrowed them from a neighbor since I had no even half-way decent shoes to wear.

I was staying in the apartment of this "old" man. So were a couple of other young people. The "old" man's name was Ted, and he was 35 years old. I had no income, no money, no nothing, and while Ted's relationship with me consisted only of his hospitality and the recurrent "spiritual" lecture he would give to any young person who visited, I started to feel guilty that I had not reciprocated. Now there was nothing too weird about these young people coming in and out of Ted's apartment. There were several apartments on Thayer Street in upper Manhattan in which lived young people and their guests, most of them folk musicians. All of us hippies. People would gather at a different apartment nearly every night to join in the music and the merriment. Ted made it possible for me to stay there. He made it possible for me to eat. He bought me cigarettes when he bought his own. He gave me a safe place to lay my head, and I was grateful. He even gave me carfare to take the subway to a job interview and I was committed to pay him back or at least earn enough to pay my own carfare next time.

I arrived in midtown via the A-train, walked up to the building and took the elevator to the 37th floor. I was taken into a fairly large room that had some sort of computer, a large box that hummed. Computers then were new, and I presume that this one got its information from what were called "keypunch cards." I sat at a small table that had three chairs. A man and a woman entered the room and sat in those two vacant chairs. They asked me questions. I don't remember what the questions were and cannot imagine what information I could possibly provide to ensure that I would be qualified to be a "clerk-typist." They nervously left the room then nervously returned with another question. I answered it. They left the room again, and again returned with other questions and received other answers. Then I was dismissed. I knew I hadn't gotten the job. I was visibly anxious and am sure my face must have been flushed to a shade of crimson. I had failed. I knew it and the failure weighed on my shoulders and pushed my spirit down into the ground.

Still, there was a drop of determination left and I dug into my purse and pulled out a couple of dimes for phone calls. I grabbed a Village Voice newspaper and began looking through the "help wanted" section. I had hardly any skills or work experience. I was a very young 20. I found an ad for a waitress and called the number. I was told by the man who answered the phone that I could come over now, and I was given the address. Like I said, I was a very young 20, very naïve and gullible. The address in the West 40s should have been a neon warning, but in a fog of depression I opened the door of a business called "Jack's Three Ring Circus." I froze. There were three large tables. On each was a woman in a g-string and tasseled pasties dancing and undulating her sexual parts to the delight of a few old men looking up at them. A man, I presume Jack, came over to me and explained that I would be a waitress. I didn't have to be nude but it would be good if I wore a leotard, and for this I would be paid $30 a day. $30 a day plus tips seemed like a small fortune to me at the time and I agreed to return the next day. I just wanted to keep my options open. I tried to talk myself into it, telling myself that if I just worked a couple of days, I would have enough to fund the furthering of my job search. My mental state grew darker and darker. My feet grew heavy with the weight of my depression and I just had to get home.

It was about 5:00 p.m. now. Rush hour in New York had fully taken hold and I could not bear to go underground and be subjected to the physical crush that rush hour in a New York subway so well delivers. So I took a bus. The bus went all the way to the northern-most tip of Manhattan, near the street I lived on. To my surprise, however, the bus route ended on the other side of Fort Tryon Park, home of The Cloisters. Fort Tryon is a narrow strip of park stretching north to south on the very northern tip of Manhattan and would take only minutes to walk across. August 30, 1974, at about 6:20 p.m., the sun was shining. It was the time when people get home from work and walk their dogs. You could hear people, some yelling, some playing, some laughing and the sound of dogs barking, the sounds of summer delight in the park on a beautiful late afternoon in late August.

I got halfway down the path when suddenly a tall young man jumped out of the bushes. I presume he followed me and managed to take a couple of minutes to remove his pants. He had a triangle of black elastic framing his privates and I wondered if he was wearing a black jockstrap backwards. He had on a short-sleeved cotton button down shirt, white socks and black shoes. Nothing else.

I screamed. He immediately covered my mouth and I struggled to breathe. I did manage to pry his fingers open a bit and said "please don't. I have asthma." Truth is I don't have asthma, but I thought this might convince him not to cover my mouth and nose so tightly. It was hard to breathe. I didn't know how or if I was going to survive what was to happen but I knew it wouldn't be good. I promised him I wouldn't scream so he released his grip on my mouth. At least I escaped that discomfort. What would happen next? I felt my peripheral vision start to close in on me. I thought I might faint when I heard a voice in my head warn me not to. If there was a way out of this, I wanted to find it. I could only find it if I stayed present. My vision returned to normal and I promised myself to pay very focused attention to what was happening, no matter how horrible, in the hope of finding an escape.

There had been a young woman recently who had told some friends and me a story of how she had been raped. She had asked the rapist if she could use her diaphragm and then cooperated with him. The moral of the story, as she told it, was that she walked away. He had not beaten her or killed her. She walked away. She walked away. And here I was, determined that somehow I might walk away as well. So I cooperated.

The man asked me questions, as if he was trying to be conversational. How old was I? "Sixteen," I said. I lied hoping that a lower number might dissuade him. Was I Jewish? "No." Was I Italian? "Yes." And quickly he was done and thankfully, was letting me walk away. I asked him for my panties back and he somewhat reluctantly took them out of his shirt pocket and handed them to me.

It took about 4 minutes to complete the walk through the park. I still remember the sounds of the birds and the sounds of children playing as I exited the park onto Broadway. How could such beauty and such horror exist in the same time and space. I was dazed. My friend Darryl and his wife lived just across the street from where I exited the park. I rang their bell and they let me in. I told them I had just been raped and they called the police.

The police arrived and took me into their squad car. We cruised the neighborhood looking for the guy; we did not see him. Then they took me to Columbia Presbyterian Hospital.

This was one of the most ecstatic moments of my life. No one around me seemed to understand that, or if they did, they seemed to think it was strange. But it wasn't strange. I was absolutely ecstatic that I was alive. I was elated that I had not been beaten or knifed. I had experienced the greatest fear of my life; a vile and ugly death was potentially imminent and I had been silently desperate. I had been helpless. But I had survived and the sense of relief I felt was enormous. I was thrilled. Joyful. As I said, I was absolutely ecstatic.

I was sitting on an exam table in a curtained-off room, and I was wearing one of those stupid exam gowns, the type that ties in the back if, in fact, you could reach it to tie it. A nurse, an Irish nurse with a full-on Irish brogue was holding my hand. I was so happy to be alive, which was contradictory to what people expected. A young male doctor who had probably had way too long a day poked his head in between the curtains and asked, "what is this patient here for?" "This little girl has just been raped," the nurse answered in a beautiful compassionate and lovely Irish lilt. "So you're waiting for an ophthalmologist?" asked the doctor. I started to hysterically laugh; could life be funnier? He left not even waiting for an answer.

Two women from New York Women Against Rape entered. I briefly told them what happened and gave them Mona's phone number; she was the girl who had lent me the sandals. We had planned to have dinner together. I asked them to call her, but PLEASE, don't tell her why I couldn't make it. Just tell her I wouldn't be able to make it and that I would explain later. I was offered and accepted the morning after pill and injections in each butt cheek, pre-emptive for gonorrhea.

Upon arriving home, it was obvious that Mona had been told that I had been raped. Now the entire group of hippie musicians knew and many of them were waiting at Ted's apartment to try to console me. I was, to everyone's confused amazement, happy, and I was also hungry, so about ten of us went around the corner to Dyckman Street to have dinner at the Cuban Chinese restaurant. I don't remember much of dinner conversation but at one point, Carol, the self-appointed "Earth Mother" of the group and most popular woman in this community started speaking to me. "I am angry with you," she said in an irritated tone. "You should be angry that this happened to you. You should be really angry." Well, I had never spoken up to anyone in the community because I had always felt peripheral, but I did that evening. "I should be really angry, you say? I'll tell you what. When you get raped, YOU can be angry!"

The pre-emptive shots for gonorrhea caused unbearable pain in my lower back which woke me at about 2:00 a.m. and kept me from sleeping the rest of the night. The pain was so bad I could barely walk.

The next day the police picked me up and drove me to the station to look at photos. I recognized no one. I had told them the man was tall, about 6'3". "Really? That tall?" "Yes," I responded. Then one of the detectives told me to watch him walk back and forth. "Was he as tall as me?" he asked. I answered that the man who raped me was about one inch shorter. He turned toward his partner and said, "I am 6'4" in stockinged feet." You see, I had paid attention. I had memorized everything I could about the man. Blue eyes, extremely short, light brown hair, thick lenses in black-rimmed glasses. How could I ever forget?

Later that day I ran into a guy named Steve as I took painful baby steps down Thayer Street because my back had been so messed up because of the shots. He came over and had this pained face of feigned sympathy. I told him I was okay, but that my back hurt a lot because of the shots they had given me. His face totally relaxed and the look of concern evaporated. It seemed as if he was disappointed. Would he have preferred the pain to be a result of the rape?

13

Willie

I aspired to be what I thought Carole was, fearless in what still was a segregated and racist world. I imagined having two children and a thoughtful, educated, handsome and politically attuned brown-skinned devoted husband. This seemed like a calling, a step forward into a world so genetically mixed between the brown-skinned and the paler skinned, that all the best traits would blend together becoming the generation of the future. I wanted to have a family better than my own family had been. I wanted to be a more conscious and more loving mother than my mother had been to me. In so many ways, though, I was still a child who believed that a mother had a fountain of energy to serve her child's needs and wants, and was supposed to be perfect. I had never considered that mothers can tire. I had never considered that their youthful experience of life shaped their adulthood and of course, their motherhood. They were supposed to be perfect and anything less than perfect seemed like a pitiful dereliction of duty. *Their* sin.

I met Victor, a young Puerto Rican with a soft afro when he was 18 and I still 17. His voice had already developed into a rich deepness reminiscent of radio announcers, and he knew he could easily use its effects to manipulate people. He manipulated me. While we were at least of equal intellect, I followed him and let him make the decisions. He had a boldness and loved to challenge the status quo, as I eagerly hid behind him as I had once hidden behind my mother's skirts. When his boldness challenged boundaries and upset people, I would disown his actions and seek shelter in neutrality. He wrote poetry, as I did. He drew, as I did, but his hand moved the pencil with full confidence and he overshadowed my art, even in my own eyes and made me ashamed of my tentativeness.

My commitment to fairness and justice has always been a part of me, even in my youth. Sometimes that commitment did not serve me well. Girls flirted with both Frank and Victor. Frankie would flirt, but only behind my back and he slept with a few of the girls, only to confess and make promises he ultimately would not keep. Victor, however, was unabashed, and would entertain the flirtation even in my presence, hoping to inspire insecurity and jealousy in me. While I did feel both jealous and insecure, it was somehow more important for me to stick to my guns, as they say, and stand by what I believed.

Girls would flirt with my boyfriend, but it was not the girls who had made the promise to me. It was the boyfriend whose integrity crumbled and was destroyed by temptation he found impossible to resist. Each of them had slept with other girls. Frank would confess, apologize and beg for another chance. Victor would get caught and emit a nervous laugh, feign an apology and use his deep, almost professional voice, to dismiss the seriousness of the charge. I would, except for the last time, relent.

It was not long after I moved to northern California that I met Willie. He was an African-American man 35 years old, about 14 years older than me. He told me that he had opened a home for the elderly after leaving his job at a hospital in San Francisco, where he had been the head of a department. Part of me knew he was lying because, after a very short time, it was clear that his mother ran the rest home. He had lied and claimed that he had appointed her to that job to give her something to do in her retirement. I was so very much estranged from my family in all practical ways and so enamored of my dream of my two brown children, that I pretended to myself and bought into Willie's stories, hook, line and sinker. Willie wore very thick glasses, so thick that it was impossible to look into his eyes and recognize any aspect of the person behind them.

99

We moved into a tiny cabin behind the rest home and spent nearly every moment together. For me, it felt so good to imagine I had people to belong to. For him, it must have felt very good to own someone, to control her and not allow her to have any thoughts or feelings outside of his direction.

We would drive up to Sam's house in the car that was in reality, his mother's. Sam lived in a tiny country house on a small vineyard that had belonged to his grandparents. He was an 18-year-old of Italian descent, one of a set of twins. Sam was the unlucky twin. He was clumsy while his brother excelled in sports. He was not socially adept, while his brother enjoyed great popularity. He wore thick glasses, his eyesight being so poor because his twin brother had managed to absorb the majority of the nutrients when they were in utero. Sam's parents had allowed him to live here in this country house on his own in the hope that independence could boost his self-esteem while he lived, at last, outside of the long shadow cast by his brother.

Sam was a good kid, a little sardonic in his sense of humor, observant and kind. Willie and I would go up there, smoke a little pot as most young people did in 1976, and "shoot the shit." Willie and Sam seemed to get along and for me, once again, there was a sense of the normality of having friends. Belonging somewhere.

Willie and I would argue, although I cannot imagine why, since I shrunk in his presence and always followed his lead. He would invent reasons to be jealous, claiming that I was looking at some guy, some guy I hadn't even noticed in the adjacent car. He never hit me but he would back me into walls yelling at me. It was a familiar feeling. I was trained from childhood to shrink and defer, unsuccessfully willing myself to disappear and awaiting desperately the end of his tirade. He would pick fights for his own entertainment and instead of yelling in my face as my fourth-grade teacher did, that I was stupid, he would yell, or whisper a threat that *"someday, somebody's gonna kill you."* Somewhere in my gut I listened, even as I pretended to myself and to him that I loved him and that there was no reason to doubt.

One day, I felt pregnant. My period was only a couple of days late which was not terribly unusual, but my nipples swelled and were very tender. My skin felt alien, like I had somehow beamed into this body. I was vaguely nauseous all day and had no interest in food. Willie took me to the clinic, but the pregnancy test came back negative. I told the doctor that I

101

knew I was pregnant and we agreed that it was, perhaps, a little too soon for the pregnancy test to show it. But I knew. I knew.

Willie and I went about life as usual and the next day; I began to spot ever so lightly. About 4:00 that afternoon, I suddenly felt a huge pain, which I have always compared to feeling like a watermelon had been shoved up my rectum. I was doubled up in pain as I climbed into Willie's mother's car as we rushed to the emergency room. Willie did as he was supposed to do in an emergency. He flashed his lights and beeped his horn but the car in front of him just saw that he was Black and assumed he was just trying to dominate the road, demanding everyone in front of him get out of his way. That driver didn't recognize that these were the actions a driver was supposed to take in an emergency. He jammed on his brakes, a very dangerous move because had Willie not been adept in getting around him, our car would have rammed his at a very high speed and we might all have been killed. I don't remember having or using seat belts, so I was jostled badly in the passenger seat.

We successfully veered around him and drove off the freeway into the hospital parking lot. Seeing into the Emergency Room from my passenger seat, it was clear that it was a busy afternoon. I asked Willie to drive up by the clinic to see if I could be seen more quickly there. As we drove into that area of the parking lot, I saw the doctor who had seen me the day before walking among other clinicians. I asked Willie to stop the car and managed to run straight to the doctor where I collapsed in front of him. I was immediately admitted.

The resident doctor, Dr. Heckey, suggested that I either had an ectopic pregnancy or a gangrenous ovary. I assured him that I knew that I had been pregnant but that the pregnancy symptoms had now subsided. The new pregnancy test was negative and it was decided that I would be taken into a small operating room where a needle would be inserted up through the cervix to draw blood. Then they could ascertain whether my spotting was my menses or if I was hemorrhaging. As they prepared the room in which to do this frightening procedure, I called my mother in New York. "Mom, hi. I thought you should know I am in the hospital. I have a good doctor and I am going to be okay. They have to figure out if I have a gangrenous ovary or an ectopic pregnancy." It was perhaps 8:00 p. m. in New York. "Oh, that's a shame. Well, let me know what happens but remember the time difference." I felt abandoned, totally on my own more than I had ever been in my life. I had reached the bottom of her shit list and I just didn't matter anymore. She didn't even ask for the name or the phone number of the hospital. I hung up the phone and cried hard but silently, as they wheeled me into that small OR.

I was hemorrhaging. They planned to do exploratory surgery the next day, expecting that it probably was an ectopic pregnancy. Cutting into my abdomen and examining with their own eyes was the only way to know for sure. I was shaved and prepped first thing in the morning, wheeled into the formal operating room and put under anesthesia. I woke up slowly and was very groggy. Dr. Heckey explained that it was an ectopic pregnancy in the right fallopian tube. He had to remove the pregnancy and the tube, but he was able to leave the ovaries intact. He told me that my fertility would probably be affected by this loss, but that he had examined the left side and it appeared that everything was fine. He said that there were cases where a woman had only a right fallopian tube and only a left ovary. Somehow the egg managed its way to that opposing tube, got fertilized and properly attached itself to the uterus. Somehow, in these cases, a normal baby was born. Encouragement it was, as much as he could muster.

I was in the hospital four days total and told to rest for the next thirty, not to lift anything or even do light housework. Just rest.

Willie's mother kept reminding him that I was the one that needed to rest. He didn't need to be in bed with me all day. She was a proud and dignified Black woman. She was strong and independent. But she felt useless in motivating her son to do anything to take care of himself, albeit take care of me. She was overprotective and controlling. Controlling she was. Protective, well, I was the toy she allowed her son to have to keep him on the straight and narrow. I gleaned by paying attention to their conversations that he had been a pimp. She referred to "his time away," which, at first, I puzzled over, not willing to accept the obvious truth. Willie told me that he had been married before and his wife accused him of killing her brother. The two were getting high, no specific drug given but I gleaned it involved a syringe. According to Willie, her brother had overdosed after Willie had left. Then somehow, the house burned down. His brother-in-law's body was found in the ashes.

Willie sported a bad wound on his right shoulder. He told me he had been shot during the war. Half the shoulder was gone, leaving only bumpy scar tissue and a slight bit of muscle covering the bone. Somehow, it never seemed to impede his movement. I asked his mother once what happened to his shoulder. I think she had started to take pity on me and although her answer was less than truthful, she simply stated that no one knew. Only Willie and his ex-wife. They were the only ones in the room at the time.

105

My gut began to ache emotionally and urged me to listen to what I knew to be the truth. Willie's angry threats that "*someday, somebody's going to kill you*" resounded in my mind and I knew that that somebody would be Willie. That someday came sooner than I could have ever expected.

14

The Axe

Theater is in my blood. I can act. Thankfully.

I pretended everything was okay. We fought, as usual, as Willie found ways and means to be jealous. He backed me into walls and yelled in my face. On one occasion I hid from him behind cars in a parking lot and had to panhandle money to take the bus back to our town and walk the mile or so "home." But then we'd make up, and as with just about every dysfunctional and violent relationship, the sex was good. Now in a hiatus from sex while healing from the surgery, there was no reward for either Willie or me. Reality was laid bare by reality itself and I began to conjure up thoughts and strategies for escaping. I kept them completely to myself. And I acted. I acted the girlfriend, pretending nothing was wrong in the face of nearly every horror Willie delivered until I could take action for real. Until I could leave.

We drove up to Sam's house and as usual, smoked some homegrown pot. Just hanging out and talking this and talking that, we laughed over silliness and pretended everything was just fine. Sam mentioned Harbin Hot Springs. I had been in a car with someone as we drove by Harbin Hot Springs and he had pointed out where it was. I, pretending to be knowledgeable, said I knew where it was. What I didn't know about Harbin Hot Springs since I had actually never been there was that it was a country spa for nudists. Willie started to yell at me. "*You fucked him up there, didn't you! Didn't you! You fucked him up there!*" I cringed and became as small as I could, unable to escape his angry accusations. Every time I would deny those accusations, he would only get louder and angrier.

Sam's little country house was warmed by a wood stove. Beside the wood stove was a box filled with small pieces of firewood. On top of the box was an axe.

"*Answer me! You fucked him up there! Didn't you!*" I tried to answer that I had not gone into Harbin but just drove by. I tried to answer that I had never had sex with the driver of that car. I tried to answer. I tried. Suddenly, Willie reached down and grabbed the axe and continued his rant. "*I know you fucked him up there. Tell me. Tell me the truth! You fucked him up there, didn't you?*"

My face grew hot and my entire body trembled not just with fear, but with a knowledge that each breath could be my last. I was about to die a horrible and horribly painful death, my head split open by the sharp edge of that axe propelled by a rage that was truly unprovoked by me, but from which there was to be no escape. "*You fucked him up there! Didn't you! Didn't you!*"

Suddenly I heard the cocking of a rifle. Willie's eyes darted to his right while his arm was still raised over my head with that axe ready to strike. Sam's rifle was aimed right at Willie. Willie put the axe down and began to apologize, explaining incredulously that he had had a flashback from when he was in "Nam." I don't believe Willie was ever in Viet Nam, or in the service at all for that matter.

I pretended to believe him and we drove home.

The next day, I "cleaned the closet." What I was really doing was organizing my clothes in such a way that no one would know but me. Everything next to the green dress was to be hurriedly packed. I was going to escape. Escape all the way back to the East Coast because clearly, had I managed to stay anywhere within driving distance, Willie would have found me. And he would have fulfilled his intentions.

I called Carole when Willie wasn't home. I told her that the relationship was bad, indeed violent and that I had to leave. I asked if I could stay with her, just until I could find a place. She was in her second marriage by this time, and although things were not going well, she agreed I could come and sleep on the couch. I knew there was no home in New York with my mother or any of my siblings, so I was grateful to have Carole's couch. I'd be safe.

With Willie not home, I snuck downtown to the post office and felt relieved and fortunate to find my unemployment check of $66, which I promptly took to the bank and cashed. I walked back home, packed the bag with everything I had planned to keep, sadly leaving that green dress that I loved behind. I called a cab which took me to the Greyhound station where I boarded a bus to New York. $50 for the bus ticket, and 25 cents for the subway, left me enough to buy enough food for the 4-day trip.

15

The Wandering Woman

It was about belonging. That's the only excuse I can think of. I didn't belong in school. I didn't belong to my family. I didn't even belong to my mother. Nobody belonged to me. Nothing belonged to me and I belonged nowhere. I cannot imagine why else I would cling to a psychopath.

I knew in my gut from the get-go that Willie had been lying to me. However, I preferred to believe him rather than my gut. It was as if I had painted my windshield with the scenery I wanted my life to be and would drive as if that was the truth. If the road of reality curved, I ran myself full speed headfirst straight into reality and then blamed reality for its cruelty. Many of the events of the past were circumstances I found myself in, but this was one of my creation. It perfectly reflected what I thought I deserved. I thought I deserved lies because the lies told a nicer story, both Willie's lies and my own lies to myself. When the truth began to be plain-out

111

screamingly evident, I still tried to ignore it and believe the story I told myself. And I did believe it, up until the time it nearly cost me my life. It was thanks to Sammy that I am still here.

So I took my $50 Greyhound bus back to New York and had nothing to do for four days but think. What a goulash of thoughts pervaded my brain! I was addicted to the illusion I had cast in front of my own eyes. I was addicted to the body in my bed, both to sex and to its sleeping presence. I was addicted to the notion of love, despite the fact that for me, none existed. It seemed that none existed for me anywhere. The stew was stirred within me, and it was clear it was up to me to make my own new start. I had to build myself from scratch. There was no one I could depend on. No one. So I had to learn, at 22 years of age, to depend upon myself. A page got turned by what would have been a horrifying tragedy and a new chapter began in which life mattered. My life mattered.

Carole was kind enough to lend me her couch, but three kids and a troublesome marriage made it clear that I could repay her kindness by getting out of there and on my feet, somehow, as soon as possible. Looking in the local paper, I found an ad for an attic room, no boys allowed, that would, for the first time in my life, be a refuge, a home.

I began working as a receptionist, bought a few new items of clothing that I needed for work and aspired to perform my songs and my poetry. I rented a small theater on the lower west side of Manhattan and performed. I virtually twisted the arm of everyone I knew, everyone I met to come to the event. I placed an ad in the Village Voice. I typed up and xeroxed programs and sold tickets for $3 per admission. I performed. Financially, I might have broken even. Spiritually, I had fulfilled a purpose. I sang my songs and performed my poetry to what seemed like the world itself. Michèle, the artist, stepped out into the world. I validated myself, despite the fact that my shyness had me sing every song with my eyes closed and my poetry was recited as I stared off into space.

> *there was a wandering woman.*
> *she knew all, but couldn't find it.*
> *looking onward, she became herself.*
> *learning not to look away, she became what she saw.*
> *becoming herself, becoming what she saw,*
> *she saw herself in all.*
> *after all, she was all.*
> *before all, she was.*

For the first time, I had made a promise to myself. I was going to keep it.

16

The Trial

I found a room. It was a miracle. I wanted to be safe and I had to be independent. I was on my own and I knew how lucky I was to find it. It was in Bay Ridge, Brooklyn, a house. Grandma and Grandpa lived on the first floor. Tonie, her husband and three kids lived on the second floor, and the third floor contained four separate rooms and a simple bathroom, each room rented to one young woman. No boys allowed! $30 per week. No kitchen, but there was a hotplate and a couple of small pots, plates and basic silverware. I never made use of them and lived mostly on won ton soup and slices of pizza. It was Brooklyn, after all.

I felt defeated, needing to return to New York after nearly losing my life in Northern California *twice*, each of those times avoidable. Each of those times was the result of choices I had made, choices that I had hoped would lead me to become a different person in a different life. And then of course, there was the rape up in Fort Tryon Park. I had been afraid I'd be killed then, but that time, I can honestly say, had not been the result of any foolish or reckless behavior on my part. That time was truly being in the wrong place at the wrong time.

I was emotionally exhausted and utterly broken in spirit. I had wanted a different life. I thought I would find one in California; I thought I would find myself there. And I did. I found that the person who had mistreated me and devalued me the most was myself. I was the protagonist in my own theatrical drama. I constructed this extreme and colorful melodrama, in which I would tilt my head to the side, stare off into space and sigh when considering what I had been through. I had romanticized my own victimhood. I bought my ticket to hell and marched willingly right through its gates. I directed the drama, cast the characters, and wrote and acted in a tragedy I thought I'd be proud of. But I was not proud. Something inside me trembled at the thought of continuing on the way I was. I had come close to the possibility of an imminent and painful death three times, and I realized I was tempting the odds. I looked up at the ceiling and spoke out loud to God (an unusual thing for an atheist to do). My exact words were, "I want you to know I am paying attention now. So could you *please* stop!"

116

Too many unbearable things had happened since I was three years old and I had grown proud of my scars. Now, however, my perspective had been reshaped after seeing the very real potential of death, not once or twice, but *three* times.

I found an 8-5 receptionist job and despite my proclivity for lateness, I arrived early every day. I bought myself a small wardrobe of new clothes for the first time in my life. (I had been a thrift shop queen in my very hippie days of poverty.) I opened my eyes and my heart to change. And the room. No boys allowed. Ever. I was safe, safe even from myself.

Beginning to have a small sense of accomplishment, I began to heal. I heard of a short-term sublet — a sublet right across the street from Fort Tryon Park and near Thayer Street in upper Manhattan where all my folk-music-playing friends still lived. So I moved there to reclaim the neighborhood and my right to live there.

It was two years minus one week exactly from the day I had been raped and that day, coming out of the subway in northern Manhattan, I looked to my right only to see the man who had raped me. I crossed busy Broadway and ran to keep up with the long strides of this man who, it turns out, was 6'3". He never saw me, and I didn't see where he went when he turned the corner. Looking down the block I noticed the small hospital. I went in and described the guy to the receptionist. She said "yes," she knew him, said his name, and told me he had gone to the fourth floor to see his mother. I asked her to call the police. She asked why and I told her.

A slew of cops and a couple of detectives arrived and escorted me to one end of the fourth floor. They brought him out of the room at the other end of the floor and asked me if that was "the guy." It was. And he was arrested.

First, I had to appear before the Grand Jury. The Assistant District Attorney, a young man by the name of Mike Acciani, instructed me on how to testify. I couldn't say "he raped me." Rape is a legal definition. I had to say "he put his penis in my vagina." I had never even uttered those words before, being 22 years old and still blushing and giggling at the use of street terms. I mustered the courage and did what needed to be done.

Again, I had to utter the same words at a pre-trial, and again at trial. The man who raped me sat there in front of me sort of in a stupor. I had to point to him and say "that's the man who put his penis in my vagina." I was encouraged by

Mr. Acciani to guard against a nervous smile which was my natural reaction to being so very embarrassed.

The defense attorney then questioned me. "Did you look for the man who raped you when you were in California?" "Yes," I responded. "Did you expect to see him in California?" "No," I answered. "Then why would you look for him there?" "Because I always wanted to see him before he saw me." I told the truth.

I was never really committed to this process. The man who raped me committed no actual violence to my body. It was clear to me that he had some mental illness that seriously needed to be tended to. I do remember screaming and he held his hand over my mouth. When I agreed to let him "make love to me," as he called it, when I cooperated, he performed his act and let me go. I still question that had I been a bigger person within myself, had I said "*no*" more emphatically and with more self-assertion than I had been able to summon from the shell of a soul I was, if he might he have stopped. Putting him on trial and then in jail never seemed to have any real relationship to resolving this broken man's issues that he contaminated my body and my life with. There was no other choice, no other avenue. He couldn't be allowed to do this again, and since I hadn't the backbone or

119

the know-how to fight back during the incident, this was the only way to fight back. Determined, I was, to tell the truth and let the outcome occur how it occurs. I had no desire for revenge and there was no possible restitution. My battles with life, the emotional scars left by this rape and my sense of vulnerability would continue to challenge me. No one could do anything about that but me. I decided my testimony would include only what I could actually picture in my mind. I did not want to add or subtract from the truth or cloud it in any way. Truth was the only proof I could offer. I did not seek revenge. The opportunity to find or create closure seemed like it was dropped in my lap and I had a duty. To tell the truth. Nothing but the truth. Thus, when the defense attorney asked if the man who raped me wore glasses, I responded that he did. When the defense attorney asked if they were prescription glasses, I hesitated, considered, and answered, "I believe so." "You believe so?" he retorted almost sarcastically. "Why would you believe so?" "Because," I stated, "I remember studying his face, trying to commit it to memory. And when I looked at his eyes, they were distorted through the lenses of the glasses."

He was convicted and got ten years, which did nothing for me except to reassure me that I had done what was there to be done. I had stood up, told the truth. Regrettably, this was the only action available to me, the only stand. The jury had done the rest.

I have heard it said that rape is *always* a violent crime. I question the veracity of that statement. The man who raped me had shown no desire to see me suffer. The fact is, nor did I desire to see him suffer. In today's world, he might have been able to get on any dating site and find a woman who would be willing, and perhaps would even enjoy, walking through a park to have some man jump out of the bushes to have sex with her. Perhaps he would have fulfilled this fantasy of his without forcing himself on someone, that someone being me. Yet I must say he indeed *raped* me, because I screamed and whimpered "no." That didn't stop him. So indeed he had sex with me against my will.

17

Echo

who are we?
lost in a void of self-creation, we are
two branches, shaking in the wind
tapping on the windows
only seeming to converse.

two clouds molded into one by the wind.
but when the wind blows again
there are no clouds at all.

two bubbles, popping simultaneously
within a murky pool.

two fools bringing to each other
gifts wrapped in creative colors.
these same two fools
can see no more than the colors.

who are we?

two diamonds in a cave.
"there is no sparkle inside a dark cave,"
say I to you.
but you cannot touch me.
I am only an Echo.

I stayed on Thayer Street for a time. I got a job at Gerde's Folk City as a waitress, working primarily for tips. Folk City had long passed its season of being the center of a social and musical movement and of cultural transformation. But folk music was still played, as were other genres and musicians like Paul Butterfield and Phil Ochs were still booked there. I was allowed to play my guitar, sing my original songs and recite my poetry during the band's breaks and on open-mike night, even on the nights I was working there. People *listened* to music then, paid attention to the lyrics. Poetry was recited, too. I imagine that much of the positive attention I received was that I looked younger than my actual age of 23, and had an innocence I never would have admitted to. Yet some of my writings were deep, filled with some sort of wisdom way beyond my years, intrinsic to life itself, ever timeless.

Taking the A train north at night, getting off at Dyckman Street and walking the two blocks and then five flights in an empty hallway to my shared apartment was terrifying at 3 or 4 in the morning. New York always seemed dangerous when I was out and no one else was around. It always seemed a real possibility that an encounter with one ill-intentioned person could mean my demise. There had been an aftermath, a change in me, after being raped in Fort Tryon Park. I had an awareness of my vulnerability and my inability to defend myself. To some people, I was prey and no more than that. That debilitating awareness infected my cells and I forged ahead despite my grave fears.

Before working at Folk City, I had done some temping, stuffing envelopes and the like, in Manhattan. Tall buildings were filled with hundreds of hurried people, and me, ghostlike and invisible. We stepped into elevators that lifted us to inconceivable heights, identified by the numbers on the elevator keypads. I rarely saw the heights I rose to physically because all of us "worker bees" were confined to cubicles in the middle of the floor, sequestered from the people that "mattered." Those people had offices with windows. A life's achievement.

I remember stepping into elevators and pressing, oh, say, the 42nd floor, only to be compelled by my fear to step out of the elevator when a few men, and men only, in their perfect suits and ties and blank expressions, would enter. The times I dared to ride the elevator with these businessmen was sheer terror. I couldn't help but see in my peripheral vision their hands reaching to unzip their flies. The fact that they stood in that stupor stare that we all have when riding an elevator, and that they took no notice of invisible me did not diminish my terror. Fear consumed me and I endured it. There was no way to escape it.

I loved wearing my white jeans and leather sandals in the summer. When I would get home, my feet were black with city sludge and so were the bottoms of my white jeans. I began to hate New York: the dirt and the danger, the mosquitoes that feasted on you at 3 a.m. in the summer, the slush that disguised itself as snow so that when you stepped off the curb, you were submerged mid-calf in mercilessly cold ice water. I hated the anonymity and the thousands of scurrying people reminded me of the scurrying roaches at Josephine's. The skyline lost its magnificence in my mind and appeared like tombstones reaching upwards out of the squalor. I was depressed.

I was depressed, and I was certain there was something wrong with me. I was, as my father was, defective. I was not like other people who knew how to be happy. I lived in constant fear and I lived in a community of musically talented hippies with a hierarchy that seated everyone else comfortably at different levels, all of which above my head. I was broken and I was despondent.

Then I met Nadine. Nadine came from France. Nadine had what I had never seen in anyone else. Nadine was confident and would simply blurt out, "I don't like this." Nadine made choices. I had never known choices were available. My mother modeled a lifestyle in which what life imposed was simply to be endured. As she did, I did. I endured. I worked, despite my fear. I never sought counseling because I never knew it existed. I never sought to improve my life because a better life was simply not part of my paradigm. *Bite your lip, bite your tongue, deal with it.* That was what I did.

One spring day I had a thought come to my mind. Maybe I wasn't depressed. Maybe I was just unhappy and didn't want to live this way. Maybe I had a choice! What a revolutionary thought! And what did I have to lose?

So Nadine and I thumbed our way cross country to California. I stayed in California only about a month, with no skills and no way to earn money, and no one and nothing backing me. I had not yet learned to stand up on my own two feet.

When I returned to Thayer Street, little had changed. I still saw the same pathetic girl looking back at me from the other side of the mirror. Somehow, though, I knew that I just had to rev up for the next effort.

I moved in with Abby into a small one-bedroom apartment. I slept in the bedroom among her possessions. I had few of my own. Abby was a student at NYU. I had barely graduated high school. I was a truant and a poet registered at Midwood High School which was heavily invested in its good stats. Thus, although my overall scholastic average barely climbed to 55 out of the 100, which was the ultimate goal, they sentenced me to an extra year, then graduated me. Now here I was, living with a New York *University* student going for her Ph.D. At moments I knew I was her equal. I could definitely hold my own in a conversation and even in a game of Scrabble, but I could grasp neither the height nor depth of my own intelligence. A little light leaked into my dark and dismal cave of negative self-esteem, and I began ever so slightly to trust myself. I began to trust my instincts.

I wrote more poetry. Some of that poetry was quite good and still holds its own today. I wrote more songs, too.

Abby invited me to see a play at NYU. We went, but I paid no attention to the play at all. I watched the Sign Language interpreter stage right and could not get my eyes off her. American Sign Language was barely introduced to common culture at that time and it mesmerized me. It was the dance of poetry itself. I pulled my courage together and went up to talk to the interpreter after the play. We exchanged phone numbers and got together sometime thereafter. Her name was Linda Bianchi. Linda was a very exacting young person. Her handwriting was tiny and perfect. She was selective, very much so, and by what seemed a miracle, after reading my poetry, she selected me. We formed a team, calling ourselves, "Echo." Our introduction at any performance was that I, Michèle, would initiate the sound and Linda would repeat it in American Sign Language, so everyone could hear. It was outstanding. Back in the day of coffeehouses, one would sign up for a 15- or 20-minute set. As you waited, you watched and listened to the artists who performed before you. As I mentioned, during this time in the 70s, people actually *listened* to poetry and lyrics. Echo, however, had something special: a melding of two young women and their distinct methods of communication that was breathtaking. I would sing or recite, and Linda choreographed her ASL interpretations with the grace of a dancer. People commented that they would almost forget that I was there. It seemed like the sound of my words, both spoken and sung, came from her, illustrated by this glorious language of beauty, grace, and a specificity that seems to come directly from the soul. We could end up performing after a rock band, a time slot that any folkie would dread, and have the attention of the audience in the palm of Linda's hand, so to speak. And it was all my writing, all my words, all my perceptions about life, my declaration to the world. We performed at New York University as well as the Henry Street Settlement and many other places throughout New York. We were also filmed at a studio at NYU for a half-hour television show, aired several times on the NYU station.

I rented a theater for our performance. I worked so hard for each performance. That was all I talked about. I told everyone I knew, *everyone* I met about it, inviting everyone and none had the courage to disappoint me.

We did a show and named it Bridges, as requested by the bass player I had booked as the opening act. I had such an inner understanding and hunger for theater that I designed and "directed" this show. It was held in a dance studio in the West 20s in Manhattan. There were rolling hassocks which we lined up for the audience to sit upon. Javier's bass lay on its side at the front of the theater, the stage area. The lights went out, and a spotlight so dim was aimed directly at the bass. You could see only its silhouette. After a pregnant silence, someone entered the dark theater and walked up the aisle to the bass.

You could barely make out his shape as he walked. You heard his footsteps and your ears followed him as he walked to the stage. Javier picked up his bass, played a few notes, leaned his bass upon his shoulder and lit a cigarette. The light of the match as he lit the cigarette flooded his face, revealing his strong black eyes and a large, sculpted Borinquen nose. Javier placed the cigarette into the strings just above the first fret and began to play a few scales. The music drifted from scales to melody to an improvised jazz solo. It was beautiful. By the time he finished his solo, the spotlight was brightly focused on him. He began to address the audience. He was supposed to have welcomed them, discuss briefly his love of jazz and of the bass, and introduce his singer. Instead he spent a full twenty minutes lecturing them on how unfair life was that, he, with all his talent for playing the bass, had to work an 8-5. It was miserable. The audience was filled mostly with my friends, coworkers and acquaintances and they were being shamed because Javier did not have the life he thought he deserved. Then he introduced Margaret, who had a strong and beautiful voice that lent itself so beautifully to jazz ballads and torch songs, unless, however, she was on stage. In live performance, she couldn't find a single note where it was supposed to be. She sang four songs, flat and sharp and nothing in between. It was miserable and I was humiliated. That was Act One.

The second act was a young man by the name of José Luis Valdéz. He was a gentle and beautiful soul. Born in what was war-torn Nicaragua, he felt it was everyone's responsibility to stop the misery which was occurring there. He sang like an angel, introducing his original songs with his beautiful Nicaraguan accent, and then carried us all off as he sang his songs completely in Spanish. It didn't matter whether we understood his words or not; he sang from his soul which he offered to us. We accepted and it was exquisite.

Then came Echo: my presentation to the world delivered on a silver tray by Linda Bianchi. I had my first perfect moment in life.

Act One was a nightmare, but the show was redeemed by José Luis' heartfelt expression, and then Linda's and mine. Phew!

Echo was a beautiful collaboration. Linda's personality was very different from mine and yet there was a flow that Echo produced that had grace and poignance. It was a jewel that I didn't know how to value, since I knew not how to value myself or my life at that time. I sacrificed that collaboration. I was young, conflicted, confused and unversed in the nature and flow of life. I couldn't ignore how much I hated New York and left for Santa Fe, telling myself that if I could have a career in ASL, my life could be a contribution. But the School for the Deaf in Santa Fe had no use for me, and Albuquerque spit me out.

Onward to San Francisco.

18

Chai Tea Latte

I stood, seemingly motionless, and yet still floated upwards straight into my ascending gaze. Between the skyscrapers was a small piece of spring-blue morning sky, and there, faint and pale, like a whisper, was a tiny crescent moon, a secret to behold by any who cast their gaze upward, as I did, with eyes open to receive the world and allow it to enter the mind. The escalator carried me further upwards, out of the BART, and I savored the few seconds of intimacy (this mingling of moon and me) until I reached the top and then began to move in rhythm with the downtown pedestrian pace.

Soon the moon no longer existed, nor did the sky, nor even the tops of the buildings. I was walking desire, beckoned by breakfast pastries and the aroma of coffee from the take-out cafés that litter nearly every corner in downtown San Francisco. I selected my café carefully, as if it mattered, as if it were really significant, and because I have always loved to be different, ordered chai tea latte with soy milk. No one flinched in the café; this is San Francisco, of course, and nearly everyone who would venture to create cappuccino or lattes in this great city is an artist. Baristas Café understands me, I think, and I sip my cup of acceptance as it warms me within.

Nothing is ordinary. Not when I remember that I am breathing and that I do not need to remember to breathe. It is a miracle. Step on the accelerator and the car goes. A miracle. Step on the brake and the car stops. A miracle. Step onto a platform and the train comes (eventually). A miracle. The doors open. A miracle. People exit. I enter. A miracle. There is a seat; I sit down. A miracle.

19

Pro Temp

I arrived, chai tea latte in hand. Time to wake up and function. Be part of the machine. I worked "temp" for years in San Francisco and Oakland. The "round peg" that had floated up from the BART in her existential dream of life had then to fit into the square hole. I could type really fast. Over 100 words per minute. I could spell. I could edit. And I could do so with the author's voice (often an attorney, usually a man) droning on in my ears as I transformed their boring sentences into a proper form to be read by another attorney or be filed by the court. Seated, trying not to slump, nothing moved except my fingers on the keyboard; nothing passed through my mind except that meaningless droning. Legal documents are filled mostly with the jargon necessary to fulfill the requirements of procedure. Rarely do they tell any kind of story. I was owned by the dictation, mind and body both. This is how I spent my days. My soul grieved its loss of life as I glanced upward at the clock waiting for the hours to pass when at last, 5:00 o'clock would declare me free. Free I was not, not yet, as I travelled home on that BART train, again deprived of the fresh air my brain so heartily craved. I am sure I have typed thousands of documents of various lengths in the 25 years or so I worked for attorneys, sacrificed thousands of hours of my youth as I struggled to fit in a life where I did not belong.

I did not know where I belonged. I knew I was an artist, and at this point, clearly would have been of the poor, starving genre had I not learned to earn at least some money pretending to be part of the mechanism of a law office.

Working "temp" meant working short stints, just long enough to amaze the office staff with my skills. I learned a lot going from office to office. I chose to work particularly short stints so that the office dynamics and dramas never seeped into my head. If they did, I was doomed to depression as I sunk into a conflicted reality I could neither figure out nor fix. Nor was it my own. I was a character actress who took my part too seriously. After a few years I began to realize that danger and learned to avoid it.

It prepared me, however, in more ways than I can count, for a future I could not have predicted. I had unwittingly sentenced myself to twenty-five years of this "incarceration."

I travelled to different locations, showing up the first day and declaring myself to be "the temp." They often cringed when they first saw me, expecting someone who was temping simply because they were unqualified and couldn't keep a full-time job. They were soon surprised, often within the first hour, because working at so many locations gave me the opportunity to master many different word processing programs and be familiar with a variety of types of law. I was never flustered at what needed to be typed into a legal form or how to type a heading on a legal brief that needed to be filed in this court or that, this county or that. I was competent. I was their magic wand.

I enjoyed having this ace up my sleeve, but it was, at best, a distraction from who I truly am: a creative person. I forced my brain to work in a way it was not really designed to. I was good at learning various word-processing programs because I had a knack for languages. My hands are rather capable, so to keep up with dictation, I ultimately learned to type about 120 words per minute. My race to type fast was the result of my desire to get this work completed as soon as possible, to see it behind me. It was an illusion I dwelled in knowingly, because in reality, I knew that as soon as I had completed typing one dictation, there would be another and another and another. I was organized, oddly enough because I am lazy. I struggled to reduce my need to focus my attention to read the words on the printed page and comprehend what I read. So I created systems to handle the filing, systems to call our attention to a particular case and sound an alarm to be sure we wouldn't miss a statute or be tardy in answering a letter. I did this over and over and over in many of the law offices I worked in. Organizing the office was a challenge I was happy to meet. Anything that would diminish the amount of tedious work was fine by me. On more than one occasion, my organization reduced the workload and thusly, I organized myself right out of an almost comfortable assignment, say, easy to commute to, and onto the next nightmare.

I had to force myself to be there, force myself to abandon each beautiful morning. Some mornings the sun promised the entire day would be delightful, and some were gray, with moody skies and pouring rain. Secretaries, being of a lower class, are relegated to the middle of the room in these offices. We were sequestered into cubicles. I felt entombed alive and by mid-morning, I felt brain-dead, lifeless, spiritless. I longed to find a way out. It took a long time to do so, but I eventually found it.

20

Transformation

S omething had to change. I couldn't bear it anymore, but looking around my world gave me no inkling of what I could do next. How could I support myself and not sell my soul?

A friend told me about a course she had taken and suggested I take it too. Feeling pushed by her in a direction I had no interest in, I declined, recoiled, deflected, hemmed, hawed, and went to an introduction but gave it no attention whatsoever. I felt strong-armed by her. She seemed to deliver an incessant and intolerable sales pitch. Ultimately I agreed, deciding that spending the tuition on the course was at least an investment in myself, and any investment in me was desperately needed.

The course was called the Landmark Forum, and the leader literally promised that everyone, all 120 of us, would complete the Forum having had a breakthrough. What did that mean?

It seemed a ridiculous, empty promise, and I was determined that I was not about to join this "cult." I can't say I completely got what the leader was communicating, but I did leave the course believing that something more was possible for me. When the leader asked the group what was now possible that wasn't possible before the Forum, I responded, "a job I like." Frankly, I didn't even believe it when I said it. He responded, "why stop there? How about a calling?" I sat with that thought as if I had never heard that concept before. A *calling*. What could that possibly look like for me? It would look like not working in an office *ever again*, but what would it actually look like. I had no idea, and I continued to muddle through my mundane existence day after day knowing I had work to do on myself, but not really seeing any clear path.

In a subsequent seminar, I discovered my habit of staying noncommittal, keeping myself distant from the things I was doing, remaining peripheral and insulating myself from outside challenges. I was telling myself I was an "individual." If I started a class that didn't meet my hopes or expectations, I would merely stop going, without any communication. Just stop showing up. If I went to a party, I would not ride with friends. I would take my own car so that I could leave when I wanted. My whole life was a refusal to be a part of anything, a refusal to see things through to their natural conclusions. I had never belonged anywhere it seemed, and my declaration of individuality made it seem as if not belonging was *my* choice. Determined as I was to have a fulfilling life, I challenged myself for the duration of the seminar (about seven weeks more) to complete anything and everything I started. I decided to accept all invitations instead of politely declining, my avoidance masquerading as free will. Now I promised myself I would alter the way I participated in my life, stepping up to the plate, being a full-on player on the court of my own life, at least for seven weeks, just to see what I could learn. I thought that perhaps, if I did things differently, then my life could be different.

By sheer accident, I discovered my calling. Carole's daughter invited me to a surprise party for Carole's 50th birthday. I began to say no because I lived in Berkeley and the party was in New Jersey. I was apt to decline invitations without even any consideration, but instead, I found myself saying yes. I had to fly to Newark Airport, rent a car, etc. to attend. Going all that way, I thought, meant that I should not just be one of the throng yelling "surprise!" I don't remember any actual thinking that led me to say what I said. I simply blurted out, "well, if I have to go all that way, I won't go just as me. I will go as the hired clown!" Where that came from, I will never know. I had never seen a clown at a party, and at that point in time, it was not common to have a clown at a child's party. I made my grand entrance, blue wig and whiteface and a costume put together from inspired rags from the thrift shop. I knew that I had turned a corner. There was a new life waiting for me. And all I really had to do was just show up.

21

Buki the Clown

(Pronounced "Boo-Key")

Being Buki the Clown presented me with the opportunity to do everything I had always dreamed of doing, plus, all my temp work prepared me for the travel and showing up at places I'd never been before, working for people I'd never met before. I got to do live theater and work with children, making them laugh. What could possibly be a more fulfilling existence?

Upon returning home from the East Coast, I immediately called an entertainment agency and asked them what I needed to be able to do to be on their roster of hired clowns. Whatever it was, I knew I would be able to do it. "Do a couple of magic tricks, some face painting and make some balloon animals." Children's entertainment was not yet in vogue in the Bay Area, so it was not yet imperative that I do those things well.

There was little competition and even the agency did not have high expectations. I, however, felt I needed to deliver to the children a show that they would talk about for weeks, months, or perhaps even years to come. I felt that I needed to learn to do the best face painting possible, so that the painted children would look in the mirror and be enthralled by themselves, and I needed to make balloon animals that they would actually play with, not hand off to their parents as they ran off to play. This, it turns out, was my calling, and I had to always do my best.

My very first party was an hour booking and there were only a few kids there. I was serious about doing a good job, but my seriousness was more evident than was my commitment to the children having a great time. I stayed there, doing the few magic tricks that I had learned and doing them badly, painting simplistic designs badly, and struggling to make balloon animals for nearly two hours, when it was just supposed to be a one-hour performance. As I packed up to leave, I remember the 4-year-old birthday boy asking, "Clown! Clown! When are you going to do funny things, Clown? When are you going to do funny things?" I got paid and slinked away knowing I had failed even my own expectations. It weighed heavy on my shoulders and I promised myself that I would never fail like that again.

This was my "dues," one might say. I paid the price with my humiliation and regret. The problem was that I had been too serious. I was fully committed to doing a good job but I didn't yet realize what doing a good job as a clown would mean.

It is challenging to walk into someone's home or backyard and entertain children you have never met before. It is a challenge to deliver a performance so inspiring that the parents know they have gotten their money's worth. It is a challenge that now I quite easily meet. It is easy to make kids happy because they want to be happy. It is their natural state. I show up with light makeup now and my hat keeps falling off my head no matter how hard I try to keep it on. Suddenly, my audience of 3 or 300 starts to laugh, and I keep prompting them to laugh and laugh and laugh again. As a result, my life matters. I have a purpose. I play. Children love to play and they love to play with willing adults. Psychologically, I become 5 again, my sense of humor is 5 again, and I feel inside like I did before life changed and became an unfixable problem. Children love to laugh. Children love to love. I inspire their love and they inspire mine. My most precious moments in life have been the ones in which I have shared my fully open heart with children. I give myself over to the moment, being everything the moment asks me to be.

I have frightened a few kids in my first months of being a clown until I learned how to wear my makeup so I do not present as a threat. I regret the fear that I inspired. It was the opposite of my intention. To those I have frightened (who are all grown now) I am truly sorry.

At the end of a working weekend, I needed to go to the supermarket for a few items. I considered going home and changing into street clothes, but I knew if I did that, I would be too tired to go back out. So I went to the supermarket dressed as a clown. There is a duty one has when being in the world as a clown. That duty is to stay "in character." So I walked down the aisles of the supermarket playing a little "clown peek-a-boo" each time I saw a child. When I had all the items I wanted to purchase, I got in line. In the adjacent line was a boy of about 4 years old. I did a magic trick for him (I'd grown better at them) and all the adults standing around beamed as they watched his delight. Then, it was my turn to put my items on the counter and as I placed my last one, this young boy said in a loud voice, *"A clown uses toilet paper!!??"*

The moral of the story is that I don't have to be funny. The children are. Naturally. And I reap the rewards of having an authentic life because I get to play.

22

Human

Our parents are human. It took me a long time to understand that. I thought my mother would have supported me, backed me up, been concerned about why I was struggling with school and failing. I thought she should have always "been there" for me. Supposedly, that is a parent's job. But the factors that created her vision of life, her vision of herself, her expectations of the world and what she thought she deserved were set long before I was born. She gave what she had, and she didn't even have enough for herself.

After having a failed relationship in my mid-30s which I wholeheartedly wanted to succeed, I realized that I had been a tangled mess my whole life and it was time for me to begin doing the untangling. That became my mission. I was in no position to have a relationship. I was clingy, insecure, and in a panic each time I reached for what I thought I wanted. I chose men who were unavailable due to everything from their psychopathic tendencies to their addiction to high achievement. In simplest terms, they didn't want what I wanted. They wanted the opposite, whether it was because of a calling they felt they had to follow or their own personal and psychologic damage that they were drowning in. Plus, our culture provided guidelines for relationships in its songs which encouraged avoidance of commitment in the guise of freedom. I sang along with those songs, but couldn't get my heart to go along with them. Women were free to have sex when and with whom they wished, our culture said. Our new social norms were incongruous with what I felt in my heart. They did not at all reflect what I truly needed. I betrayed myself each time I had sex with someone I was infatuated with. They didn't care about me. They couldn't see me for who I was and I was completely blind to them. I was composed of shattered aspects and conflicting parts of myself, a self built of reaction and fear and horrible self-talk, without redemption. I was a shaken-up pile of odds and ends, each with its own character of misery. How could anyone understand me? Even I couldn't.

My parents tried to be good people, tried to be good parents. My mother had a dream that life did not live up to. She never knew how to navigate her life to a place where she didn't have to constantly fight for survival. Her strength was endurance, and she had no vision of a life she might actually

150

desire. She never raised a voice of hope, intention or creativity. She was deeply talented at gritting her teeth and surviving the storm. My father was at odds with himself. He betrayed his dreams and each time he gave them hope he would fail miserably. He thought himself a weak man, and his desire to make himself happy seemed to him to be an addictive hedonism that sabotaged him and made him ashamed to be who he was.

In a letter to my mother from his stay in Syracuse, he wrote:

Honey, I am deathly afraid that we are not going to make it. What am I going to do? I am so completely alone and miserable, and when I do come down to New York, I can't get the opportunity to get close to you. Somehow my failing to make a go at driving the cabs discouraged me and you know me, when I discourage, I discourage way down deep, where I can't talk myself out of it.

I shouldn't tell you this because I don't want to discourage you. You've got a tough enough job. You're feeding the kids on the pittance I've been sending you. God knows how probably you must eat yourself. So, as I say, I shouldn't tell you this, except that in telling you it acts as a purgative; and in sharing my burden with you

151

while it's still a problem to be solved, I can carry it better and perhaps solve the problem while it can be solved, rather than confess a fait accompli.

As far as the job itself is concerned everything is great as yet. That is if I keep going in steadily and I will from now on, headache or no headache.

Well, I'll close. I hope I'll be in a better mood tomorrow.

Love,

Pete

I grew up with the stories my mother told me. My father was flawed. So it made sense that I was, too. The passing years, life experiences, self-inquiry and willingness to change, have provided me with a pool of wisdom to access. And why not be willing to change? I was miserable as I was. I was a failure through and through. If my efforts to change failed, one more failure would not alter the black hole that was my soul.

My father was not flawed. He most likely suffered from bipolar disorder, was definitely depressed, and was a food and cigarette addict. He suffered from headaches, perhaps migraines. He had no skills to navigate his life. Having the responsibility of three, then four children, he had not the freedom, the opportunity or the place to grow into his real self. He was an artist, a round peg that didn't fit the square hole, just as I have always been. It was not "character defects" that polluted his existence and inflamed his disabilities. He was young, artistic, and had no time to mediate the conflict between his artistic self and the practical one responsible for a wife and four children. He had a mental disorder, some kind of brain chemical imbalance. He could not escape his mental malady to a place of objectivity where he could fight the good fight in life. He was impotent in the struggle of a warrior and had no weapons or tools to meet the challenges of his life.

I forgive him.

I appreciate my mother who lived through the poverty times, those times when she couldn't even provide food to her children. I appreciate her pulling her four children through those times and whenever possible, allowing us to believe in our own childhood bliss. I would guess her profound fear of a future filled with hers and her children's failure to survive haunted her nights, while her children soundly slept to the music of one another's breathing.

Back in Greenwich Village, before the onslaught of my dismal reality, before the foster homes, we would cross Sixth Avenue and stand in front of Woolworth's. She would need to purchase Brillo pads, or soap, or some other necessity. She barely had enough money to buy these necessities, but when she did, she would line us up with our backs to the store window and warn us.

"Don't ask for anything. Not a sound! If you ask for something, you will definitely not get it. Maybe someday I will surprise you and have enough money to buy you something. But for now, DO NOT ASK FOR ANYTHING!"

Her face and her voice were stern, and we walked in behind her like baby ducklings, making every effort to avert our eyes to avoid the sin of childhood desire.

An unexpected consequence was that I grew up not asking anything from life, not asking anything for myself. The mere purchase of a dress, a pair of jeans or even a new pair of shoes to replace worn-out ones with my own earnings filled me great pangs of guilt. I bought a pair of Frye boots once. They were very much in style and, while a bit expensive, would have outlasted their cost by years. I saved for them from my meagre earnings. However, I could not bear my sin of indulgence and hid them in the back of the bottom of the closet. Simply viewing them reminded me of my unworthiness, despite the fact that I had bought a very practical item with my own hard-earned money. I donated them, brand new, to a thrift store, unable to alter my reaction to them, but declared that they would be my sacrificial purchase. I then declared that anything else I would buy for myself I would have the right to own; I would have a right to my pleasure. I learned that life was not a matter of having *no* choices, but is instead a series of choices, some of which are to be taken on thoughtfully, and some joyfully. I have only to be responsible for those choices. With that as the subtext, my flirtation with choice became a relationship of creativity and responsibility. Ultimately, my choices lead me to the actions necessary to achieve the results of my imagination.

I have trudged through the mud not knowing where the mud stopped and I began. I opened my eyes and paid attention to reality like it mattered. And it does matter. Thus, I have risen and continue to rise each morning grateful for another day.

23

My Best Friend

When our human brains are forming, childhood experiences program us neurologically. I believed that I was worthless, or perhaps even worse, I had negative worth. I suffered depression which underscored that belief and there were times I was very much ashamed that I was even alive. I could point to all the instances where I wanted to relinquish any personal responsibility for my desolate self-view. I could have declared myself a helpless victim. Something inside me has always refused to do that. Somehow I always knew that, whether or not my actions are the cause, I am fully responsible for my life. Something inside me proclaimed my right to be alive and demanded acknowledgement of my innate value, although it didn't look like that to me at the time. During my later teen years, I smoked pot. Many teenagers did. I also tried pills, heroin, and cocaine. How fortunate was I that I just did not like being high. Marijuana gave me a high that was sometimes wonderful and sometimes put me to sleep. It gave chocolate, particularly chocolate ice cream, a sense of royalty in my mouth, making it a full-on sensual experience, which resulted in insatiable cravings. Other times, marijuana just made me paranoid. I was afraid of other people in the room, afraid of windows and who might climb through them to harm me. I was afraid of what people thought as if their thoughts could actually kill me. I was uncomfortable in my own skin. There were also the times where marijuana made creativity seem more important than my breath. Music was three-dimensional and deep thought was an exquisite journey. I do not regret smoking marijuana for all the years I did. And because I was fortunate enough to find being high on heroin a gray, subdued, lifeless experience which I had no choice but patiently wait to wear off, it neither claimed me nor scarred me. It did not dull my emotions, but only my senses. It felt like having a fever and being weak and sleepy. I had no interest in life at all. I gratefully say that, ultimately, I had no interest in heroin and other drugs at all. I was born with a spiritual legacy which would not let me go. Somewhere along the line I learned that if I was to be happy in life, I had to learn how. I learned that it was my responsibility and no matter what the source of my emotional pain, my sadness or my trials and tribulations, this life belongs to me. It is for me to own my life. And I do.

You may wonder who my mother was. My mother was my best friend and I am clear that the times she closed her emotional doors to me was because she was closing her heart to herself. Life was challenging and demanding and she was utterly depleted of fight. She pushed herself away as much as she pushed me away. I know she loved me, although I questioned it during our difficult times. I no longer question it. I am completely grateful to be her daughter and I thoroughly acknowledge that she was a unique, intelligent and delightful human being.

My mother was a highly principled woman. The only two men she was ever intimate with were my father and the father of my younger brother. She would never have broken her vows had she not been pushed completely to the edge. Even my father acknowledged that, and as he put it, "*I pushed you into it, Toni.*" As my father avoided reality because of his mental illness, he avoided work. He didn't show up to run the Italian hero shop that was ours. My mother would feed us, clothe us, and bring us to school, and then go to the hero shop to find he had not opened it. So she did. She tended to the cooking and the serving of customers. She had to manage the employees and place orders for supplies. At the time she had the affair that resulted in my brother coming to be, my parents were way behind in rent. Eviction was imminent and she was desperate. I believe Steve's father comforted my mother and that comfort went further than she had ever intended it to go. I believe that she hoped this new man would step up and step in to handle what was unhandleable and turn things around. Instead, pregnancy resulted and turned a terrible situation into an even worse one. My mother told me that she applied for Welfare at the time and at her interview was told that they could offer her no help because, *"you have a husband."* She was utterly hopeless. It was 1959. Her despair elicited actions she never would have considered otherwise.

Ultimately, after all was said and done, she got her favorite son out of the deal. She raised him differently than she raised her three oldest children. He never wore second-hand clothing. His bad behavior was tolerated. His childhood was far from perfect, but he was in receipt of a kind of coddling we never knew existed. Not that we three older children ever minded. We all coddled him, too.

24

Shampoo

I buried my face in my hands, carefully keeping the washcloth on my eyes, as my mother washed my hair. She was extremely careful, proving a point to her mother, who was not there. No shampoo ever got in my eyes, and I swooned into the lovely head massage, water temperature carefully tested, each stroke of her hand meant to please. I am sorry I ever grew up to wash my own hair. I miss my mother and I miss that bliss.

My mother washed my hair so kindly because her mother had scrubbed her head like it was an exorcism of dirt never choosing to see her daughter's pain in this process. Yet my grandmother loved her only child completely in the only ways she knew how to love and my mother knew it.

My mother's description of her getting her hair washed as a child talked just as much of my grandmother's beauty as it did her cruelty. She said,

"One of the worst experiences of my young life was having my hair washed. My mother's hands were beautiful, long tapered fingers, well-shaped nails, these were hands which should have been adorned with precious rings. But, except for a gold band on the third finger of her left hand, they were not.

On hair washing days, these hands would change identities. I would cry and plead not to have my hair washed. Fingers would dig into my scalp in order to vanquish the dirt there. Very often shampoo would sting my eyes. My poor eyes, the casualties of war, red from shampoo, swollen from crying."

I am, and always will be a student of life, contemplating what makes us do the things we do. As we move step by single step through life, life comes at us in breezes and bursts of wind. We experience emotional paradise, hurricanes and tornados. We stand up to the rough weather as best we can, and it marks us forever, scarring us with hardship far more than last the good memories of how we may have danced contentedly in the moonlight or awakened to the glorious symphony of birds.

I know my grandmother struggled. She built a wall of thorns around her and thought nothing of sending malicious and mean barbs your way, even when you were an innocent

162

child. Yet somehow I always knew that she was a tender soul within. She had somehow mustered steel for nerves, simply to endure what had been her everyday life. She loved me. I know it, but she didn't understand me in the least, and everything about me that she didn't understand was an affront to her. Her love could only be shown in the perfection of the dresses she sewed, from precious remnants she saved for just the right time and just the right person. Sometimes that person was me.

My mother's and my grandmother's blood runs in my veins. I have learned from them, less from their intentional teaching and more from observing what I know had been youth and hopefulness in their early years, their warrior-like struggles to meet the challenges of their lives, and from the somewhat defeated people they became in their older years. I, too, had been young and hopeful. I, too, struggled like a warrior. Now I am who I am in my older years. I have learned to value joy and communication. I have learned to apologize for my mistakes and to forgive others and myself. I have learned that freedom to be oneself is independent of the circumstance of the moment.

163

25

The Land

I had never thought of it as a retreat, not knowing what a retreat was, nor really having any clue as to what staying in a country cabin would be like. It promised to be an adventure, and it was. It was an adventure in which time slowed down, and after a couple of days to dispel my fidgeting, I did too.

My friends Peter and Briana owned this land, way up in the northeast of Mendocino County. We drove through town and then took an unmarked road up to their land. They had two cabins on the land, one larger than the other. The larger one was where we stayed. It had running water they finagled through hoses from one of their four streams. Two were assured to dry up in the summer, but with luck, the other two would continue to offer their pure, cool water.

Other friends stayed there that week, too. We all basked in this new reality, one so very different from the city doings that made up the texture of our lives. It did not take long for me to realize that this was in no way a retreat from reality. It was a deeper, more complete experience of life. It required little of me to stay there, but required everything of me to be there. I had to give up all my longing to be distracted and busy. I received its warm sun and its cold night air which enveloped me. I sensed the truth of the earth. I sensed the personality of this mountain where we stayed.

We were up perhaps three-quarters of the way to the top of the mountain, and although we were very much to the east of that county, the fog came all the way in from the west, where the Pacific Ocean offered its truths, too. The white milky fog floated in from west to east, and we watched and witnessed it, as we sat above it in the warm sun, grateful to avoid its chilly touch.

There is a natural self in all of us, one which we, who have lived in cities all our lives, barely get to know. Nature happens up here on this mountain, and we are subjects to its whims, as it wakes in us a truth of who we are. We are the revelation. Life is suddenly more real than we ever knew it could be. We are present, and we are free to dream. Our instincts assure us that we are well acquainted with this place we have never been to before. I would happily skip like a five year old child

166

from new facet to new facet, thankful that this experience of nature was so colorful and so kind to me.

I loved the feeling of the sun's warmth on my skin. It felt personal, as if that sun reached out intentionally with its delightful touch. As well I loved the contrast of the fire, its loving warmth, reaching out to comfort me in the cold of the evening. We were far up the mountain, looking out over a valley to another mountain. So thick were the trees on the other mountain and so few were its human inhabitants that no lights appeared in the dark night to announce the existence of their night fires. I felt like we were alone on the planet, alone in the comforting arms of Mother Earth itself. It was as ancient an experience as it was new. I was mesmerized by the billions of stars that twinkled at me as we shared a wordless conversation, these stars and I, an acknowledgment that they saw me as I saw them. What a gift!

We built a small sweat lodge, bowing branches that had been sacrificed from the manzanita trees and laid all around this land, free for the taking. They arced and crossed each other until they made a 360 degree dome, over which we layered blankets upon more blankets. At its center, a small pit was dug into the ground where we placed rocks that had been heated in a well-fed fire for hours, removing them from the fire with pitchforks and placing them at the center of the sweat lodge. Pitchers of water had been filled by the nearby stream, which was generously adorned by wild mint, and when we poured the water on the red hot rocks, the steam that sizzled up was fragrant and delightful.

We took turns in the sweat lodge, three of us at a time. I shared the experience with Peter, whose son called him "Father Peter," (my father's name) and another friend. The sweet minty steam seemed to enfold us and comfort us. We chanted improvised syllables of joy and pleasure and completed our turn exiting the sweat lodge satiated and somehow very gently spent. I had hoped to have a mystical experience, and it was, my senses so present to my body, and my body so present to itself.

I climbed into the loft bed where I slept in the cabin, as friends lay sleeping and snoring on their futons on the floor. Dreaming and waking were, it seemed, two sides of the same coin.

There was a knock on the door. Only I heard it and climbed down the ladder from the loft. I walked to the door and opened it. There stood my father, Peter DeLuca, the father that had died about twenty-five years earlier. He was slightly out of breath and sweating profusely on his forehead and face. I bid him enter and got him a chair to sit on. "Daddy! Daddy! Sit down!" I dipped a rag in the cool water that came from the faucet in the cabin's sink. I wiped his brow with that rag, almost out of breath myself for suddenly there I was with this man that I belonged to 100%. He was my father and I was his daughter and suddenly, out of the magical darkness of the night, here we were together. He began to speak in a breathy voice. "I had to come back. I had to tell you I am so proud of you. You have grown into an intelligent and beautiful woman and I love you. But now I have to go. I have to die."

With that, I was sucked away from all senses of him, as I rose out of the depth of my sleep, not knowing for a few minutes which was sleep and which was wakefulness. I sobbed without knowing I was sobbing, until the sound of my cries brought me further awake, although my heart yearned for a way to reach back into that dream or that other awakened state, whichever it was, to see my father and talk to my father again. I longed to gently wipe his face with that cool cloth again. I wanted so deeply to embrace him.

Returning to a familiar reality, somehow, I was forever changed.

Epilogue

A Handful of Raisins In an Otherwise Empty Room

I was dropped into a dark hole. Nothing around me but strangers. Nothing familiar. I was only a spectre when I was noticed, and I was noticed rarely. I always heard my heartbeat in my ears and I studied every moment, keenly aware that although food, clothing and a warm bed were provided, my survival was not ensured. I was five years old and I was on my own. Every night, when handed those raisins, I had a moment of intimacy with my own soul. I could control how slowly I ate those raisins, savoring not just their sweetness, but the sweetness of a few moments when I was alright.

Writing this book was the easy part. I'd mentally step into the moment of life I was remembering, look around and describe. The words would simply come to me. They expressed what I noticed. It was like visiting myself at another time. I experienced a catharsis, even as I felt the loneliness and sadness of the past. The resulting emotion was comfort. I had the experience of comforting the young child I once was. I looked back and validated her, creating an illusion that she was never really as alone as she felt. Thus, I transformed the experience of that five-year-old as that experience lives in me now.

That five-year-old transformed her own experience, having within her the desire and the instincts to be happy that I believe every child has. Receiving a handful of raisins while she lay in bed, the sun still bright in the evening sky, she made joy of those raisins and she made that joy last. Existing in the lonely and frightening cloud of separation from her mother, her father, her brother, her sister and the home she had known, she created a silver lining. She owned those moments; she experienced a handful of joy in an otherwise empty, lonely and sad life, and she made that joy last.

Bullied and devalued by a teacher and by members of my family, I believed I lacked any worth. Yet there was a glimmer of light. Somewhere in my conscious mind, I continued to consider the world, what it was, and what was possible in life. I knew there was happiness, and unsure if I was worthy of any of it, I remained attentive. I reached out for the *handful of raisins.*

I tried drugs, but thankfully, did not enjoy them. They did not offer me the escape they offered so many young people, so many of my cherished friends, so many of whom didn't survive. *A handful of raisins*, I might say, beckoned me, and pulled me through.

I loved in a situation where love simply could not survive. I descended into a life which could only deteriorate, barely surviving and suffering. But I did not want to miss the *handful of raisins* that somehow I knew existed outside the small, sick circle I was living in. There was another life. I had to find it. I had to change. I had to find joy. I had to create my own *handful of raisins*.

Becoming a victim of violent crime, I still saw myself as greatly fortunate. I was desperately afraid for my life and of the potential for pain. None of the things I feared with all my heart and soul occurred. I lived. The sense of relief I experienced was immense and my *handful of raisins* was the heightened joy I experienced of being alive. Nothing makes the preciousness of life so apparent as when one thinks she is about to die.

Being alive is an absolute miracle, whether I notice the miracle or not. Being alive with class. Being alive fearlessly, despite fear itself. Being alive fully, truthfully. Being a contribution. Being present and being grateful. Celebrating the fullness of my life, I seek and accept the *handful of raisins in an otherwise empty room.*